2/21

LIVING THE RICHNESS OF THE CROSS

John Dalrymple

AVE MARIA PRESS
NOTRE DAME, INDIANA

ACKNOWLEDGMENTS

Jonathan Cape Ltd. and the Executors of the Estate of C. Day Lewis: "Walking Away" from *The Gate* by C. Day Lewis.

Hutchinson Publishing Group: "Marble Floor" from *Collected Poems* by Karol Wojtyla © The Vatican.

Scripture quotations are from the *Revised Standard Version Common Bible* copyright © 1973 by the Division of Christian Education of the National Council of the Churches of Christ in the U.S.A.

International Standard Book Number: 0-87793-273-5 (Cloth)
                                       0-87793-274-3 (Paper)

Library of Congress Catalog Card Number: 83-70945

Printed and bound in the United States of America.

First published as *The Cross A Pasture* by Darton, Longman and Todd Ltd., 89 Lillie Road, London SW6 1UD.

Text design: Elizabeth French
Cover design: Katherine A. Robinson

Marble Floor

Our feet meet the earth in this place;
there are so many walls, so many colonnades,
yet we are not lost. If we find
meaning and oneness,
it is the floor that guides us. It joins the spaces
of this great edifice, and joins
the spaces within us,
who walk aware of our weakness and defeat.
Peter, you are the floor, that others
may walk over you (not knowing
where they go). You guide their steps
so that spaces can be one in their eyes,
and from them thought is born.
You want to serve their feet that pass
as rock serves the hooves of sheep.
The rock is a gigantic temple floor,
the cross a pasture.

Karol Wojtyla
in St. Peter's Basilica
Autumn 1962

CONTENTS:

Introduction 7

ONE: *Christ's Work*

1. *Passion and Death* 11
   The Cross
   Approaches to the Passion

2. *Disturbance* 19
   Jesus as a Disturber
   Jesus and Today's Church

3. *Kingdom of God* 33
   Not a Lamb but a Teacher
   The Human Community
   Fatherhood of God

4. *Redemption* 45

5. *Seek First the Kingdom* 55

TWO: *Our Work*

6. *The Christian Life* 65
   Discipleship in Christ
   Prayer in Christ
   Suffering in Christ—Our Cross

7. *World Village* 77
   Political Christianity
   Village Concerns

8. *Change* 91

9. *Love, Death and Resurrection* 101
   Embracing the Cross
   Our Deaths

10. *Sharing* *115*
      Fear and Love
      Charity Ends at Home
      Prayer of Partnership

Appendix: *Prayer of Partnership* *128*

INTRODUCTION

When I was asked to write a book about Christian suffering I felt that it ought to start by considering the suffering which Christ underwent and base its reflections on that historical passion and death on Calvary, and so avoid the temptation to talk about our suffering today without reference to that archetypal suffering which gives hope to all Christians. So the first part of this book is a consideration of the life and death of Jesus. The argument is that he did not primarily seek the cross, but embraced it as the necessary station he must pass through on his way to inaugurating his Father's kingdom. The cross was the inevitable end to his mission, but the mission up to Calvary is important too, if only because we cannot understand the cross unless we understand what put Jesus there. From the beginning Jesus' universal love made him a critic of the religious authorities of his day. So, to cut a long story short, they put him to death. I am very much aware that no one writing about Jesus can hope to portray the whole man and his mission. We are bound to capture only parts, so this book does not hope to convey the whole meaning of Jesus' life. If I have emphasized one point, namely the dissident element in Jesus' love, it is because that was the reason for the opposition against him, and without it he would not have been crucified. It was the key to his suffering. He was a supreme example of the saying, If you love you will make enemies. Theologians writing about Christ today develop this insight and argue it with more knowledge than I have.

The suffering of Christ was one thing. Ours is another. The link between them is crucial for Christians. I believe that it is much more than an exemplary connection across history, that it is nothing less than an interior mystical union by which we live in Christ and Christ lives in us, and his cross and our cross become one. So the central chapter of this book is Chapter 6, where this is discussed. The last four chapters consider what seem to me four important areas in our lives in which the cross of Christ is operative and gives meaning to our existence.

7

The prime value for all Christians is not to aim at suffering for its own sake, but to aim at love, to be completely surrendered to God in our hearts. When Jesus himself did that he suffered the cross. We can be sure that it will happen to us too. Provided we are putting in the first place that surrender to God, we Christians can let the rest of our religious duties unfold themselves, not mindlessly, but in a spirit of discernment which does not turn its back on human culture but always puts God first. We can do this with trust because we know that God is the author of human culture, as well as of the gospel, and does not ask us to accept the cross as a denial of human values. On the contrary, both in Jesus' life and in ours the cross is a richly positive thing, the path to glory. For the sheep of Christ the cross is a pasture, a rich grazing ground for our hungry spirits.

I am grateful to the Sisters of the Holy Cross in South Bend and in Tiberias in Galilee whose invitations to give lectures for the last five years have stimulated me to think and pray about these matters. I always thank God for the Holy Cross connection. I am grateful to friends who have helped me; Eileen Millar, Roland Walls and Hugh White read the manuscript and made valuable suggestions. Sister Clare of Jesus typed the manuscript and corrected the proofs with her usual patient accuracy and efficiency.

—John Dalrymple

PART ONE:

Christs Work

ONE

Passion and
Death

THE CROSS

The suffering and death of Jesus Christ, his passion and cross, stand at the center of the Christian religion. The life of Jesus of Nazareth provided many graphic symbols, each of which might have been taken as the distinguishing sign of his movement: good shepherd, bread of life, light of the world, lamb of God, resurrection, transfiguration. None of these became the Christian sign. Instead, the sign of Jesus' suffering and death was accepted everywhere as the official mark of Christianity. We hang crucifixes on our walls, wear them around our necks, build our churches in the shape of the cross, put the cross on flags and medals. Almost certainly there will be a cross near the reader of these pages. It is the central symbol of Christianity and permeates our culture.

The passion and cross are also the central devotion of Christian spirituality. All Christians down through the centuries, whatever their differences, have been united in thinking the death of Jesus was the most important event of their religion, and so have woven a great tapestry of devotions around that central fact. Catholic spirituality especially, with its traditional base among ordinary people, has thrown up a large number of devotions to our Lord's passion, some of them shocking to people of taste, but all vibrant with love of the suffering Christ. One thinks of devotions to the pierced Sacred Heart, the Precious Blood, the Ecce Homo, the Five Wounds, the instruments of the Passion, the Pietà, and particularly of the Stations of the Cross and the Sorrowful

Mysteries of the Rosary. These have nourished Catholic piety over the centuries.

Behind the meditations on the sufferings of Jesus during his passion has been the conviction that Jesus Christ died for our sins. It has been this fact, surely, which has made people concentrate so lovingly on the way Jesus suffered and died. If his death were not so important, then there would be little concentration on the manner of his death. But because his death was known to be completely central to Christian life, then there arose the loving concentration on the manner of his dying. Perhaps the reason for putting all that emphasis on how Jesus suffered is that people have found it difficult to say why Jesus' death was for our sins, so they transferred attention to the easily comprehended physical details of his death. We have been told, and we believe, that Jesus' death took place to redeem us from our sins, but once that is said it is difficult to go further in devotional pondering. It is easier to accept the fact without more questioning, and then to focus on the way Jesus died.

The second conviction about the death of Jesus, in Christian spirituality, is that there is a connection for all followers of Jesus between Jesus' cross and our cross. Not only did Jesus die to save us, but also his suffering on the way to death, his cross, is linked with our sufferings, our crosses. This is another accepted truth in the Christian way of life, and again it is a truth which is easier to accept as a stated fact than to delve into and explain. What is the connection between Jesus' death on Calvary and our hardships now? Conversely, why do Christians, following St. Paul, claim that the upsets and frustrations of their lives now have a definite link with the epic death of Jesus in first-century Palestine? Once we start trying to answer these questions we embark upon theology, which baffles or frightens many of us. We prefer to stop at that point and link our sufferings and Jesus' sufferings together in prayer without further analysis. But if we love Jesus and make him the master of our lives, the question of our link with him arises insistently and will not be shelved. We want to know as much as possible about that precious reciprocal link between the death of Jesus and our own lives. In our parish we often sing:

> And when I think
>   that God, his Son not sparing,
> sent him to die, I
>   scarce can take it in;
> that on the cross
>   my burden gladly bearing,
> he bled and died
>   to take away my sin.

When I sing this verse I ask myself in what sense was Jesus of Nazareth a man sent by God to die; in what sense was he, when executed, bearing my burdens; in what sense did he bleed and die in the first century to take away my sin in the 20th century? I look across the congregation in church and wonder how each member is understanding the words. We all subscribe to them as central truths of our faith, but what do they in fact mean for us? We say that we are willing to bear Jesus' cross, but what do those words mean as we progress through the ups and downs of our lives? We ought not to take them for granted. We ought to try to find out why it is a privilege for a 20th-century person to bear the cross of that first-century person who was put to death on his cross because of the disturbance he caused to the society of his day. Many of us have often prayed these words without much thought. I believe, however, that it is important to think through the twin Christian assumptions that Jesus' death was for our sins and that his past death and our present lives are religiously linked. The pages that follow are an attempt to share my personal exploration into these questions. They are no more than a piece of a personal search among the works of theologians and spiritual writers, supported by my reflections and prayers over the years.

Approaches to the Passion

There seem to be four ways in which Christians link up
the cross of Christ with their lives. The first is to look at the
passion of Jesus and take it as an example for our lives. We
take Jesus as a model for conduct. We look at his behavior
during the passion, and it inspires us to try to imitate him.
His silent dignity before the Sanhedrin, his challengingly
truthful attitude to Pilate, his courage and perseverance carrying the cross to Calvary, the prayer, "Father, forgive
them," as he was nailed to the wood, these act as inspiring examples for us. So we lovingly run through the passion and
death of Jesus in our minds and pray that we may act the
same in our lives. This is the way in which the first epistle of
St. Peter treats Jesus' passion. In chapter 2 slaves are told to
be submissive to their masters, even when their masters are
unjust, and are reminded, "Christ also suffered for you, leaving you an example, that you should follow in his steps. He
committed no sin; no guile was found on his lips. When he
was reviled, he did not revile in return; when he suffered, he
did not threaten, but he trusted to him who judges justly" (1
Pt 2:21-23). In other words, imitate the crucified Christ.

A second way to react to the passion of Jesus is to
remember Jesus' words (Mt 25:31-46) that he is in our
neighbor, especially in suffering neighbors like prisoners, the
poor and the sick. The passion of Jesus is then seen to be not
only the historical event of A.D. 30, but also a continuing
event in the world of today. The historical Jesus was beaten,
tortured, harried to death in Jerusalem two thousand years
ago; today he is still beaten, tortured, harried to death in
many parts of the world in the person of our fellow human
beings. As Pascal put it, "Christ is in agony until the end of
time." Our reaction to the passion of Christ, then, is to keep
the historical event of Calvary at the back of our minds but to
place Christ's 20th-century predicament in the forefront.
Someone meditating on the passion along the lines outlined in
the preceding paragraph would think of Jesus as he was then
and try to imitate him now. Someone meditating on the pas-

sion in this second way would think of Jesus as he is now and try to discern his present suffering in the oppressed. The next step would be to ask where one stands vis-à-vis today's passion of the Son of God. *Am I, in the world today, acting the part of Caiaphas, Judas, Peter, the mob conspiring in the suffering and death of Christ, or am I aligned with people like the Jerusalem women who mourned, Simon of Cyrene who came to his help, the good thief who believed in him?* Reflection like this on the passion and death of Jesus is a popular modern way of praying. In his Stations of the Cross Michel Quoist prays, "Christ is still dying. He continues to offer himself to his Father for the redemption of the world through the men who today suffer and die around us." I have found this reflection a fruitful approach to Holy Week in the parish. The Negro spiritual "Were You There When They Crucified My Lord?" is a poignant accompaniment to these thoughts.

A third way of thinking about the passion of Christ is simply to go back to the events of the first Holy Week and try to relive them with Jesus. "Compassionate your Savior thus cruelly treated!" prayed Saint Alphonsus. This means entering as far as possible into the succeeding events of the passion, trying to imagine what they must have been like for Jesus. Thanks to the extensive coverage of the passion in all four gospels this is not too difficult. The Stations of the Cross have traditionally done this. Their realism, however, has been marred by the habit of seeing the passion of Christ, through the eyes of later theological reflection, as an exercise to redeem humanity from original sin and make atonement to the Father. These are legitimate reflections found in the New Testament; they correctly say what the theological meaning of Christ's death is. But to the extent that they put into Jesus' mind thoughts developed by later theology they are questionable. "He receives it with meekness, nay with a secret joy, for it is the instrument with which he is to redeem the world," reads one commentary on the Second Station (Jesus Receives His Cross). That implies a Jesus detached from the actual happenings of his passion, exercising divine knowledge of the significance of what he was undergoing, from a position outside history. The reality must have been quite different: a condemned man, his mind reeling from the events of the past few days, steeling himself to face the final steps toward execution, praying for the strength to remain faithful to the God whose fatherly kindness he had been publicly extolling for three years and who he feared might now be forsaking him, a man tempted to run away, having to exercise faith, but who was about to prove both his courage and his faith to the highest possible degree. To picture, instead, Jesus as the serene God-man with no internal struggle, physically in pain but mentally outside it all, is to step beyond history, however theologically true the meditation may be.

This approach to the passion has resulted in a divided picture of Jesus. His physical sufferings have been vividly depicted, with full recognition of his human state in terms of blood, sweat, tears and the agony of his death. But Jesus' mind has not been accorded the same human state. He has been credited with divine understanding of what was going on, with the result that much human passion and agony has been eliminated. I recall a version of the Stations of the Cross which addresses Jesus: "You are thinking about me, and that suffering seems a mere nothing to you when it is going to save me." There is nothing in the gospels to suggest that Jesus had those supratemporal and suprahuman thoughts during his passion. It is, I think, not spiritually helpful to interpret Jesus' last hours on earth in such an unhistorical way. Admittedly all meditation on the passion involves the work of imagination. Nevertheless today Christians look for a consideration of the life and death of Jesus by a use of the imagination in terms of what really happened in order to understand the events from which Christianity began. This is not easy, since the gospels are not straight historical records. We should nevertheless make the attempt to understand Jesus' passion historically. We have more chance of doing this with Christ's passion than with the rest of his life, since the passion narratives are closer to history than other parts of the gospel. They merit our serious study, since what Jesus was trying to do in his own society and how that society reacted to him were the foundation events of Christianity.

A fourth way of reflecting on the passion and death of Christ is to begin with those foundation events of Christianity and ask why the Jewish and Roman authorities conspired to put Jesus to death. What was in his life and teaching which made them do it? Questions like that place us in the middle of real events, the actual life of Jesus. From there we can try to view the passion of Jesus and see it for what it was—the execution of a social and religious disturber. We need to examine why Jesus was a disturber and so discover why Caiaphas wanted to put him away. This means putting forward considerations about the passion and death of Christ which belong to a time before they were realized to be the events which redeemed the world and made atonement for the sins of humankind. It also means not being content with the explanation that the passion happened because God "sent him to die." We want to know the human causes of Jesus' passion before we study its divine ones. Only after we have recorded contemporary reactions and tried to enter into Jesus' mind during the events of that last week should we proceed with theological considerations about atonement and redemption. A spirituality which is based on theology but not on the history behind that theology is lacking an important ingredient, and is likely to be unhelpful for people today who want to base their Christian lives on the man Jesus as he lived in history. History is perhaps not the right word to describe our knowledge of the passion. We know that the gospels are not straight history but are themselves theological reflections about the life of Jesus made by the early church. So we do not expect to find accurate historical reporting in the gospels. On the other hand we do find the *story* of Jesus there. The story of the passion is not modern historical narrative, but it is certainly about real events, not invented fantasies. That is enough for our purpose, which is to go behind the church's later developed theology of redemption in order to concentrate on the life and mission of Jesus as experienced by himself and his contemporaries.

TWO:

Disturbance

Jesus as a Disturber

The death of Jesus became inevitable after the meeting of the Sanhedrin recorded by St. John in his 11th chapter.

> The chief priests and the Pharisees gathered the council, and said, "What are we to do? For this man performs many signs. If we let him go on thus, every one will believe in him, and the Romans will come and destroy both our holy place and our nation." But one of them, Caiaphas, who was high priest that year, said to them, "You know nothing at all; you do not understand that it is expedient for you that one man should die for the people, and that the whole nation should not perish" (Jn 11:47-50).

We are accustomed to thinking of this meeting taking place just before Good Friday, and so setting in motion an immediate arrest. An interesting recent suggestion is that it took place at least a year before on the occasion of an earlier visit to Jerusalem during which Jesus expelled the buyers and sellers from the Temple and took the place over in a provocative way. This would imply planned opposition against Jesus for longer than a few days before his arrest. Whether that is correct or not, the point of this meeting is that it marks the moment when Jesus and the authorities in Jerusalem became set on a collision course which could only result in the removal of Jesus from the scene if the delicate status quo of Israel were to be maintained by those in authority. Jesus had made his message too clear, was too popular with the ordinary people, was altogether too public a figure to be ignored. So he had to be suppressed.

This collision between Jesus and the religious authorities of his day is the underlying factor of the second half of his public life. From the time he left Galilee and took his band of disciples outside Herod's territory northward to Caesarea Philippi and elsewhere, Jesus knew that his life and message were making him the enemy of the priests and scribes. He began to foretell his passion and death. He knew that for the sake of his message he was a disturber of society, and that those in authority would not let him go unmolested. Turning toward Jerusalem for his final journey was a brave, clear-sighted decision on Jesus' part.

The meeting of the council, recorded by St. John, has a ring of truth about it. I have been at meetings, sometimes chaired them, where the subject under discussion has been the threat to a delicately achieved status quo posed by an idealist. There is usually a mixture of genuine bewilderment (What are we going to do about this man?) and an equally genuine sense of responsibility for making the right decision (We've got to put the public good before other considerations. This man is a danger to the business, diocese, seminary . . .). Usually, too, there is a member who carries the meeting, as Caiaphas did, with the tough line that the idealist is too dangerous to be left alone and must be gotten rid of. (It is all very well to have idealistic notions, but one has to be practical and maintain the commonsense position.)

In Jesus' time the commonsense position in Jerusalem was an acceptable working compromise with the occupying Roman power in Israel. The Romans maintained law and order and tried to ensure the peace needed for prosperity, the *Pax Romana* of the Mediterranean world. The Romans recognized Jewish law as competent in its own field and gave the priests and scribes their important position in Jewish society. The compromise was a mutual recognition by Roman and Jewish leaders of their respective positions. Above all, the Romans allowed the Jewish authorities freedom in the Temple and did not violate that precious Jewish sanctuary. The Jews, in turn, promised to maintain peace and order in the Temple area. It was a good working arrangement. Many Jews, especially those who bore the burden of leadership, must have been glad to have achieved this somewhat precarious *pax*, even though they could never accept it in their heart of hearts and knew that they must work ultimately for the complete freedom which was their heritage since Moses. But there is a price to pay for all concordats.

What was the price? To the 20th-century mind, accustomed to the separation of church and state, the price seems small. The Jews gave up their unrealistic notions of total political freedom which, except for the brief Hasmonean kingdom, they had not enjoyed for hundreds of years anyway. But the Jews still believed that total political freedom for their nation, the Chosen People, was God's will for them. Countless prophets and heroes like the Maccabees had taught them that, and had been prepared to give their lives for that ideal, because for them it was God's purpose. The price of the concordat was, therefore, religious betrayal in the eyes of many of the devout among Jesus' contemporaries. Another factor in the compromise, which Jesus undoubtedly saw, was that it was an agreement between the rulers on both sides, which was to their benefit, but was scarcely to the benefit of the poor of Israel. Their land was occupied by Roman soldiers, and occupying forces are never pleasant or too nice about their methods. The system of taxation, operated under the Romans as a private enterprise by the hated publicans, milked the poor and resulted in widespread poverty. Undoubtedly there was oppression in Palestine as in other oriental Roman colonies. The third and worst feature of the status quo defended by Caiaphas at the council meeting was that it worked to produce a religion of social conformity. Since the return from exile in 538 B.C. the religion of Israel had become more and more orientated to keeping the Law and obeying the priests. Prophets no longer appeared, to preach a living religion to Israel. There seemed to be no direct contact with God in the official religion of the day, only contact with Law, custom and other impersonal things. No doubt many in Israel had become used to this rather dead religion, but there were others who wanted a change and longed for God to reign more personally in Israel. Among these was Jesus. He looked at the compromise negotiated by the high priests and did not like it. He was prepared to upset the delicate balance maintained in Jerusalem and went there to do so, because he thought it was God's will.

In the next chapter we will examine more closely the content of Jesus' teaching. Let us here note how completely Jesus challenged the status quo of his society by what he said and did. The way he cleared the buyers and sellers out of the Temple and his Palm Sunday procession into Jerusalem were direct challenges to the authority of the priests. Before that his preaching about the reign of God which he had come to set up must have seemed an impertinence to the religious authorities. Certainly his attitude to the Law was a challenge. He did not deny its importance, but he healed sick people on the Sabbath and had no use for the nit-picking complaint that his followers, pulling ears of corn as they walked through the field, were harvesting on the Sabbath. In other words he made the Law relative, not absolute. He did the same with the other great religious absolute of Israel, the Temple. That, too, was relative. As a devout Jew he frequented the Temple, but he also taught that all could have direct access to the Father in prayer by just praying in their secret room, and he told the Samaritan woman that a time was coming when people would worship God neither in the temple on Mount Gerizim nor in that on Mount Sion but anywhere, in spirit and truth. This was very challenging, because by making the Law and Temple relative, he made the scribes and priests less important. These two classes felt the presence of Jesus as a threat.

Very often it is not what a person says that constitutes a

threat but two accompanying factors: his manner of saying it, and his popularity with the group. We all know how we can listen to any number of complaints from persons who are unsure of themselves or who are obvious eccentrics. We take their complaints in our stride. We feel more threatened when we are challenged by someone who clearly knows what he or she is talking about and who has backing from others. What that person says makes us sit up and listen. Jesus spoke with authority, as if he knew all about what he had to say, as if it came straight from God. Furthermore Jesus was popular. He had the backing of big crowds. In the crowds were dedicated followers who fully believed him when he said he had come to inaugurate the reign of God in Israel. This combination in Jesus appears to have been devastating. Even more than what he said, perhaps, his manner of speaking made Jesus a threat to the status quo and a disturber of the delicate peace. In the council meeting in Jerusalem described by St. John it seems that it is the person of Jesus which made him the threat he was. "If we let him go on thus, everyone will believe in him." There seems to be a lot of fear in that "everyone." It was Jesus' magnetic personality that the council feared.

The reader may be wondering if I have made Jesus out to be more of a political figure than he was, have perhaps been using 20th-century secular categories to portray him. I believe Jesus was a completely religious person. His mission was religious. His whole personality was religious. To be religious, however, in Jesus' world was to be political as well. There was no distinction between the two categories. A person who broke the Law of God in Israel was committing a civil crime as well as a religious one. The person who disobeyed the secular authorities was regarded as disobeying God too. Religion and politics were the same thing. A person, therefore, who preached a religion of love and saw beyond the accepted importance of the Law and the Temple was speaking politically even as he taught religion. Was the council meeting at which Caiaphas led the members to decide to do away with Jesus a political or a religious meeting? It was both. A social and political decision was taken to suppress the Galilean disturber, but it was taken as a religous decision to please God, under the leadership of the high priest. So when we say that Jesus was a disturber of society, we do not mean that he was some sort of social agitator like a modern political activist. Jesus was a religious person who acted to please God whom he called his Father. He committed himself to a religious reform, but he clearly foresaw the dire political consequences for himself if he carried it through. Jesus was a man of prayer. The social disturbance he caused was the disturbance caused by love, and he, not others, suffered for it.

Jesus, in fact, was less political than many of the religious idealists of his day. To understand Jesus it is instructive to look at the three main types of religious idealist which were to be found in first-century Israel. The fact that Jesus chose not to belong to any of these groups tells us much about his own religious ideals.

Jesus was not a Zealot, the most political of the religious idealists of Jesus' day. They aimed for a new Israel, which would be the kingdom ruled over by God, ushered in by a Messiah who, like David, would take up arms against the Lord's enemies. Their prime aim was to destroy Roman power in Palestine. They fought for this in the manner of freedom fighters down through the centuries. They refused to pay taxes, sometimes took to the hills guerilla fashion, sometimes assassinated their enemies as collaborators with the Romans. They were single-minded idealists fighting for what they thought of as a religious cause. Jesus did not join them. He paid taxes, mixed with Romans, preached peace, kept laws, proclaimed love rather than hate for enemies. He asked people to turn the other cheek against aggressors. He was notably sympathetic to collaborators with the Romans like Zacchaeus in Jericho. He was on quite a different wavelength from the Zealots. When he eventually marched to Jerusalem, it was not to perform a political coup, but to establish a kingdom very different from that desired by the

Zealots. He had won his battle against the Zealot temptation months before. He would not let the crowd make him king on the hillside after he had fed the five thousand. He had not accepted the Devil's offer of this world during his 40 days in the desert.

Jesus was not an Essene. Some religious idealists of Jesus' day had decided that the only hope for Israel was to go apart from society in order to form ideal communities in monastic establishments like the Essene foundation at Qumran. Here they prayed and waited for the New Israel, convinced that contemporary society was damned. They lived a strict life of asceticism and ritual purity, under a rule, in preparation for the new kingdom which only they would be fit to enter. In other words, their religious idealism made them opt out not only of the Roman Empire but of Jewish society as well. Like the Zealots they adopted an extreme position. Jesus did not join them. He remained in society, mixing freely with all types, the ritually pure and impure. He was not a ritual fanatic, nor even an ascetic. He followed no rule, was not monastic in his teaching, was a great party-goer. His religious idealism did not lead him in the direction of the Essenes any more than it led him in the direction of the Zealots.

Lastly, Jesus was not a Pharisee. The Pharisees were the religious idealists of the day within the establishment. Like the Zealots and Essenes they too longed for the new Israel, but where the Zealots took to freedom-fighting and the Essenes took to monasticism, the Pharisees may be said to have taken to the Law. They found their religious ideal in the study of the Law and in the perfect following of it. That, for them, was where the true Israel lay: in the two absolutes of Law and Temple, the two God-given means of serving the Lord for all sons of Israel. Being realists, as well as idealists, they accepted, at least for the time being, the Roman yoke in their country. Meanwhile they turned toward the perfect spiritual following of the Law (which did not upset the Romans) in order to find God. Jesus, as is well-known, was not a Pharisee. He respected the Law of Moses, but did not stake all on perfectly observing it. In fact, he demoted it to a position relative to people's needs. As the Sermon on the Mount shows, he placed the religious ideal not in external legal observance but in the heart of each individual loving God above all things and loving all men and women with mercy and compassion. That, he said, was the fulfilment of the Law. Jesus was especially on a different wavelength from the Pharisees. His notion of God and the kingdom was much too revolutionary for the Pharisees. As we shall see, Jesus believed in mercy and forgiveness rather than the full rigor of the Law for sinners. He did not believe at all in the social prohibitions encouraged by the Pharisees. He mixed freely with all kinds of people and was shockingly unobservant of the religious taboos of his day.

I have made these three brief comparisons of Jesus with the religious idealists of his day to show that Jesus was not like them. He indeed disturbed the society of his day, but in his own unique way, not in the way that they disturbed it. He had other aims. Put briefly his aim was the reign of God in a kingdom of universal love, regardless of social or political demarcations, a kingdom where God is Father of all, and everyone, however small in society, matters. For that ideal he gave his life.

JESUS AND TODAY'S CHURCH

The sort of man that Jesus was and what he was put to death for poses a problem for the church in every age. The problem is embedded in the fact that the church is a two-thousand-year-old institution whose task is to conserve the teaching of Christ down through the centuries. How does a conservative institution keep alive the message of a radical reformer? How does the establishment we call church represent Jesus who was a critic of the church establishment of his day and was actually put to death by that establishment? This is a question which cannot be adequately answered in a few pages of a book. On the other hand it cannot be bypassed just because it is difficult. Any consideration of Jesus Christ by a Christian who is a church member must face the problem. Furthermore, even the Christian who has decided not to be a church member has to face the problem. He or she too depends upon the church and owes it a debt, since we know about Christ and Christianity only because of the church's presence in the world and because of the church's struggle in each generation to preserve the truth about Christ. Leaving the church does not solve the problem except in the sense the seceders no longer have to think about it. Seceders leave the church, and the church carries on without them, preserving the message about Jesus for another generation, among whom will be more seceders.

Leaving the church because of its infidelity to Christ's message is not a constructive answer to the problem posed by the church's institutionalism. Neither is the founding of a new church, aiming to return to the pure reforming principles of Jesus. The experience of history shows that breakaway movements from the institutions of the church, however gloriously free their first beginnings, themselves become institutions in a short time, one or two generations at the most. The problem recurs in that short time, no nearer solution, with the situation only complicated by the arrival of one more Christian body within Christendom. The temptation to be an essene, to gather in a pure church to wait for the new Israel, is strong and understandable, but it is not the way of Jesus. Christians must stay in the marketplace of Christianity and work for a solution there.

It is wise to recognize that there is both a continuity and a discontinuity between the church and Jesus Christ. The church as we know it is simultaneously revealing the person of Jesus to the world by her pastoral work and teaching, and hiding him by acting so often contrary to the message which he brought. There is clearly, in the first place, a theological continuity between the church and Jesus Christ. We have preserved his message (especially in that first church book, the New Testament) and we teach it. The liturgy brings the

presence of Christ and his saving work into people's lives. If I
answer a call from our local hospital and go to anoint a patient, hear his or her confession, give holy communion, I am
taking Christ to that person. At Sunday Eucharist in the
parish we are doing what Jesus Christ told us to do in his
memory, and we have a guarantee of his presence and prayer
in our celebration. In pastoral work as a priest I know that
Jesus is working through me, however ineffective an instrument I am. Because I am an ordained priest in the church,
the continuity between my work and that of Christ is
guaranteed; and this is so for *every* member of the church, by
virtue of his or her baptism.

If there is a theological continuity there is also, however,
a constant discontinuity between Christ and his church
which can best be called a discontinuity of witness. Here we
return to the problem of an institution bearing witness to an
institutional dissident like Jesus. The contrast between Jesus
and the church as it has evolved through the centuries is striking. The church is a great international body with a
bureaucracy and a diplomatic service. She negotiates concordats with Christian and atheist governments alike. Naturally
those concordats contain compromise. The church is
prudently cautious in her dealings with people both within
and without her flock. She generally proceeds with
calculated diplomacy. She is notably property-owning. Her
official representatives, the clergy, often live settled, comfor-
table lives. They aim to get on well with civil authorities. The
church as a whole likes to work for the alliance of throne and
altar. All this is in marked contrast to the life of Jesus. As we
have seen earlier in this chapter, he was not interested in
negotiations or cautious diplomacy but was an outspoken
prophet, an enemy to compromise. He lived an unsettled life
once he had begun his ministry. He was not, apparently, a
property owner. He clashed with the religious authorities
because he did not like their compromising position. He was
a layman. He was, it seems, in his style of life everything that
the average Christian, clerical or lay, is not: itinerant, pro-

phetic, risky, poor, uninterested in either his civil or religious status. To put it in modern terms, Jesus was not a clergyman working for the reign of the church, but a layman working for the reign of God in the world.

This startling contrast between Jesus Christ and the church he founded comes from two sources. The first source of contrast is simply the paradox of a great historical institution representing a prophetic founder—the paradox of Papal High Mass in St. Peter's continuing the liturgy of the Upper Room in Jerusalem, of St. Peter's itself being the beautiful civilized sign of the radical prophet who died an ugly criminal death. This paradox is not in itself sinful. It is part of the human condition. You have to have institutions to carry on a prophet's message and work. It is how humanity transmits what is best in its experience. In the case of the Son of God's message the institution is divine in origin but purposely human in its development because the Son of God became a man and chose to operate through human beings. So the church as institution, now worldwide and two thousand years old, is inevitably very institutional. About the fact of institutions there should be no difficulty. Even the New Testament has strands of prudent institutionalism in its teaching, and Jesus may be said to have laid down the plans for the apostles to govern in his name which contained the seed of the subsequent institutional church.

The mere fact of there being an institution in Christianity is not shocking. The shock is when the institution is found to be developing a life which is contradictory to Jesus' ideals. Jesus' ideals were subversive of much that was, and is, accepted as necessary by the worldly wise. Jesus parted company with the rulers of his day on subjects like religious compromise, the pursuit of wealth, the exercise of authority by domination. He did not do so quietly but in public from the rooftops. The church sometimes shows a distressing tendency to act like a worldly ruler, to want to make friends with the rich and powerful, and even to be as dishonest as some of them can be. When she does this her continuity of witness with Jesus is broken even while her theological continuity remains intact.

A striking image of how the church as institution should give a firm, uncompromising lead in the world, while preserving intact the way of Christ and refusing to play the power game, is given in Pope John Paul's poem about the floor of St. Peter's Basilica in Rome, written when he was a bishop at the Second Vatican Council. He sees the floor of the great church, not its dome or marble walls, as the significant unifying factor.

> The floor . . . guides us. It joins the spaces
> of this great edifice, and joins
> the spaces within us,
> who walk aware of our weakness and defeat.

Unlike the domes and arches of a baroque church, the floor is lowly and insignificant, scarcely ever looked at. But it is the key element for unity in the building. Pursuing the comparison the poet gives a sharp reminder to Christian leaders of the way of Christ:

> Peter, you are the floor, that others
> may walk over you . . .
> You guide their steps.

John Paul does not overlook that this way of leadership brought Jesus Christ to Calvary, and he concludes the poem with a reference to the cross, but the cross seen positively as beneficial and nourishing, not as mere denial. For the sheep of Christ it is a pasture.

The church must never be in doubt where she stands on this subject. She must not adopt the standards of the world instead of those of her founder. She must not play the world's game in order to preserve herself in being. Otherwise she might in a later generation be siding with those who crucified Christ in the first generation. Christians cannot shrug their shoulders and accept paradox here. We have to work to abolish any contrast between the style of the church and that proposed by Christ. We must work to make our manner of living a witness to the gospel of Jesus. We must make the values we stand for in our community the absolute values of Jesus, not a woolly compromise between his teaching and current secular principles. There is a lot for us to think about here—such subjects as Christians in big business, Christians in the modern armed forces, Christians who are rich, church leaders who imitate the style of living of those who have power in the world, to mention only a few matters of conscience. We, with God's help, have to model our lives on the example of Jesus, regardless of the approval of society in and out of the church and remember also his gospel warning that no man can serve two masters. There is simply no other choice for Christians—for us who have crucifixes in our homes, and who open and close our prayers with the sign of the cross.

THREE

Kingdom
of God

Not a Lamb but a Teacher

To call Jesus of Nazareth by the title Lamb of God is as old as Christianity. The Lamb standing, as though it had been slain, is one of the central moving images of the Book of Revelation. From there it has found its way into the church's liturgy. Before communion at every Mass we invoke the Lamb of God who takes away the sins of the world. Jesus, sacrificed and slain for our sins, is the message intended by the image of the lamb, and as such it has entered into the spirituality of the church. There is, however, a danger if we use this image for Jesus too much. The danger is that we may concentrate on the sacrifice of Jesus on the cross and forget why he was led there in the first place, that is, forget about the life that preceded his death and which was its cause. We may be tempted by the lamb image to think of a mindless, innocent victim taken to slaughter in order to provide a sacrifice to God. Jesus, however, was not a mindless victim, and his role was not merely to provide a body for sacrifice. His role was to inaugurate the reign of God and give us specific teaching about loving God and one another. Jesus was put to death by the Sanhedrin and Pontius Pilate because they rejected this role of Jesus. Jesus himself saw his death as a religious act of sacrifice ("This is my body given for you. This is the cup of my blood . . . poured out for you."), but those who killed him did not. For them it was a simple matter of religious and political necessity. They put an end to

33

Jesus' life because of the danger constituted by his teaching. They were nailing his teaching to the cross when they nailed him. On his part Jesus knew that he was being killed because of what he had done and said in public. He knew that his teaching was disturbing the powers-that-be in Jerusalem, but he did not change course, still less run away. In other words, Jesus believed so passionately in what he had to say, and in his being sent by God to say it, that he was ready to die rather than keep quiet or alter the message. It truly can be said that Jesus died for his mission and message. The lamb sacrificed was a teacher.

We must take the life of Jesus seriously if we are to take the death of Jesus seriously, because it was that life and message which caused his death. The Romans and Jews who crucified Jesus were crucifying his life and message when they crucified him. That is why the image of the lamb is only partially helpful. It concentrates on the death of Jesus but passes over his life and teaching, and can even give the misleading impression that his death was an isolated sacrifice which was called for by God but which had little to do with his mission. Jesus' death had everything to do with his mission; his mission provoked it. What God sent Jesus to do was not primarily to die, but primarily to inaugurate his reign upon earth. That this was in fact done by the death on the cross of the teacher-inaugurator of the reign of God was the foreseen disaster out of which God drew greater good, but it can hardly be called God's primary intention. His primary intention was to bring the old covenant to its fulfilment and inaugurate the new, peacefully if possible.

In our spiritual approach to Jesus' passion and death we too must take Jesus' life and teaching as seriously as we take his death, because they are all of one piece. When we mourn the sufferings of Jesus on the cross we should not merely mourn the physical sufferings. To mourn Jesus is to align ourselves with the mission of Jesus which landed him in those sufferings. To stand spiritually at the foot of the cross means to take a stand as a disciple of Jesus, open to his message, ready to be counted as a promoter of that message. It would be supremely hypocritical to shed tears over Jesus' passion while living a life unaffected by Jesus' teaching. It would be the equivalent of siding with Caiaphas but going to Calvary to weep over the corpse. The sufferings of Jesus on the cross were not merely the sufferings of a lamb being sacrificed for a good cause independent of the lamb's intentions; they were the sufferings of the man who actively introduced the good cause into the world and was rejected and tortured by those who feared it.

THE HUMAN COMMUNITY

The essence of Jesus' mission (which ended on the cross) was what he did and said. He himself called it the arrival, or presence, of the kingdom of God among men. He saw his mission as announcing its arrival, in fact promoting it. *Kingdom* is a misleading word in English—there are over-tones of sceptres, crowns, thrones and pomp which were far from Jesus' mind. To call it the reign of God is better, especially if we think of *reign* as a verb rather than a noun: God reigning among us. This reigning of God in the world was what Jesus committed his life to bring about, beginning by urging everyone to stop and turn his or her life in this new direction ("repent"), and then begin to live in this new way. He did this by his sayings, by his wonderful stories, and especially by his actions. At a deeper level than his words was the impact of his own person and life. He *was* the message he came to bring. This message was one, but had two in-terpenetrating elements. The first element was the brotherhood and sisterhood of all humankind in one family. This in turn depended on a deeper element: the fatherhood of God.

When he began his public life Jesus left Nazareth and went down to the busy lakeside villages at the north end of the Sea of Galilee, making his base in Capernaum. He pro-claimed the kingdom, and began an astonishing life of in-volvement with people, living, apparently, publicly at the disposal of all who came to him. Not for him the vocation of an Essene, withdrawing from the public into a monastery. He concerned himself with the crowds who inhabited the populated centers of Galilee. These crowds flocked to him, drawn especially from the oppressed outcasts of society. He did not avoid them but welcomed them and healed them. In the understanding of the day the sick and the sinners were practically identical; you were sick from leprosy or blindness, for example, because you or your ancestors had sinned. It was your fault. The sickness was a visible sign that God was displeased with you. It is hard for us to imagine what it was like to be ill or handicapped in pre-Christian Jewish society. Imagine the burden you would have to bear if your misfortune and pain were attributed to being in sin. To the physical pain would be added the psychological pain of living with the fact that God was displeased with you. Imagine believing that because of a sickness you were possessed by a devil. As well as physical and psychological burdens, sick people in that society had also to bear the social burden of being cast out of society. Devout people, observing the Law, reacted by shunning them as sinners, excluding them from respectable society. The result was twofold: a widespread feeling of inferiority among the vast numbers of these oppressed, sick people; and a division in society between the publicly acknowledged good people and the publicly avoided sinners. The greatness of Jesus was that he, a man of God, broke through this evil which was protected by consecrated taboos, and was moved with compassion to mix with the sick and sinners and heal them. The healing was more than a mere word to each person. It was the fact that Jesus sought out the company of these physical and moral lepers, affirmed and accepted them, was moved with compassion for them, sat down at table with them, and made them his friends. He restored their self-respect and encouraged them to have faith that they could be better. Then, said Jesus, your faith has made you better! This seems to have been the way Jesus' miraculous healing power worked. Hand in hand with his power to heal from infirmities went his power to heal from sin.

This friendship with outcasts was sensational. The gospels record the shock it was to the devout to see a man of God (he prayed all night sometimes; he taught in synagogues; he had healing powers from God) mixing with outcast sinners and sick people. What Jesus was doing was breaking through the prohibitions laid down by the Law for those who wanted to please God, and doing so in *the name of God*. Law-abiding Jews were not allowed to mix with Romans, the hated heathen occupying power; or with Samaritans, the heretic cousins; or with sinners. Jesus mixed freely with all three and brought them healing both physical and spiritual. It was a campaign. It was an announcement of what the reign of God meant. Jesus followed his actions with injunctions which have never been forgotten, which must have been sensational too. His followers must forgive, nay, love their enemies; they must turn the other cheek to aggression; they must love everyone, excluding no one; they must learn to see him in the outcasts of society and would be judged on the way they treated such people.

I think it is important to notice that, though Jesus' campaign of love created repercussions in his society which reached the authorities in Jerusalem and were most certainly political, he was not responsible for starting a political movement. He simply set out to love all men and women and set no barriers to this love. He consciously broke the religiously sanctioned customs of his society, but always in the interests of individual persons in need of love. Time and again he was "moved with compassion" and performed a healing. In St. Mark's gospel such an act was nearly always followed by a command to keep it quiet—not the action of a man about to found a political movement. The gospels sometimes show Jesus exercising a marked detachment from the immediate concerns of his society. He seemed at times to step aside from becoming involved in people's social problems. When he was asked to adjudicate about the inheritance between two brothers he replied, "Man, who made me a judge or divider over you?" (Lk 12:14), and then went on to talk about the evil of covetousness. He opened a vision before his audience of men and women so bent upon seeking the Father's kingdom that they ceased to be anxious about property. Jesus tackled problems at a deeper level than the social or political. He went to the sinful roots of those problems in the human heart. He did indeed found a movement and gathered disciples around him, and even sent them out to perform works of healing and preaching through the towns and villages of Galilee. But, although it had strong social and political effects, it was a radical and profound religious movement. It was the setting up of God's reign on earth. It demanded purity of heart and the spirituality outlined in the Sermon on the Mount, not mere political activity.

Jesus, then, was neither an Essene, avoiding society, nor a Zealot, trying to change it by taking up arms. Jesus had much in common with the Zealots. Like them he was clearly fed up with the way those who sat in the chair of Moses were compromising their position and allowing the common people to starve, both materially and spiritually. Sheer disappointment and, at times, anger with the priests, scribes and Pharisees boil over in the gospel accounts of Jesus' teaching. But Jesus never joined the Zealots, surely because he had more spiritual concerns. He saw that the short cut of political action offered no lasting solution to the state of the people. If an armed revolt succeeded and the Romans were thrown out of the land, the result would be a change of persons in government, but perhaps no change in the situation of the outcasts and oppressed whom Jesus loved. That is normally what happens in revolutions. The structures change and the persons in top positions change, but the hearts of the people are not changed; often they are brutalized and made worse by having been in war. Jesus went about his revolution in another way. He put God as Father in the center of it. He aimed to change the hearts of men and women religiously with the profound spirituality we find in the gospels. He preached that message and was content to let the rest follow from there. It was a completely idealistic approach, and, people being what they were in his as in every generation, it offered no chance of success. It was just not practical politics in the Roman Empire. Many in his audiences, though fascinated by him, must have thought him mad. His relatives did. They came one day to try to stop him because they thought he was "beside himself."

The gospels were written to show that, though Jesus did not succeed in converting anyone important to his kingdom and, in fact, raised the fatal opposition of the priests, his message went out far beyond the time and place he lived in—to "the ends of the earth," to you and me in our world today. The short-term results, however, were disastrous. The campaign to extend love to all persons in society raised too powerful an opposition for Jesus to be left in peace. Caiaphas held that historic meeting (Jn 14:47-50) and plans were successfully laid to have Jesus suppressed. It has been said that if you love, you will make enemies. It is a bitter insight into human nature that this is so. I remember when a priest friend, Jim, came to help out in the parish. Jim had a powerful way with people who were down and out. He warmed to our policy of welcoming them into the house, offering them food and shelter. He joined in enthusiastically. Once he came the numbers increased. Jim even sought out poor people to invite in. The kitchen began to overflow with them; tea, milk, sugar, bread, jam and cheese disappeared alarmingly fast. It was difficult to cope with the increase; the crowds about the house began to be bothersome. I began to get worried by the sudden expansion. I was shocked to find myself beginning to feel hostile to Jim, because of his powerful love. Parishioners, too, showed signs of sharing my feelings. Jim's campaign to love the outcasts of society was in danger of making him enemies. Then he left, and the crowds began to be manageable again. Jim's impractical idealism was gone, and some of the gospel with it. I discovered uncomfortably within me the truth that those who love much make enemies among religious people because of their love.

FATHERHOOD OF GOD

The call to recognize our common humanity was the more visible of the two elements which make up the kingdom of God for Jesus. The less visible element was the more important. This element, which provided the motive power for Jesus' unlimited love of humankind, was the fatherhood of God. Jesus' conviction about this was what made him supersede sacred customs and break through social barriers. God is the Father of every member of the human race; we are all therefore one family, and equality of importance and respect must prevail among all men and women. Jesus experienced God as Father in an intense, intimate way. Jesus must have inherited all the Jewish reverence and awe for Yahweh. Against that background he moved into an unheard-of intimacy. God, for him, became Abba, Dad. Out of this intimacy with God came Jesus' bold campaign to practice and preach universal love. Treating everyone with compassion and respect, regardless of past record or present status, was for Jesus not just a cherished ideal. It was the will of God whom he called "Abba" and who called him "my beloved Son."

Insofar as we can trace the spiritual development of Jesus (his "growth in knowledge and wisdom") we see that it was a series of crucial Abba experiences. The 12-year-old boy whose dawning vocation made him give his parents the slip and stay behind, fascinated, in the Temple at Jerusalem, excused himself for what he had done by saying, "Did you not know that I must be in my Father's house?" He seems to have had some special experience of God as his Father during those days in Jerusalem. Twenty years later, when he went to be baptized in the Jordan by John, the adult had an experience similar to that of the child. As he prayed he heard a voice, the voice of God as his Father: "Thou art my beloved Son; with thee I am well pleased" (Mt 3:17). This was so overwhelming a spiritual experience that he proceeded from there into the wilderness to think it over and pray. And so his public life began.

Two further key episodes illustrate the developing experience of God in the life of Jesus. His experience of transfigured ecstasy on the mountain was again accompanied by God's voice as Father: "This is my son, my Chosen; listen to him." Later in Gethsemane, not now in ecstasy but in agony, it was not the Father speaking to him, but him speaking to the Father that we hear: "Father, if thou art willing, remove this cup from me; nevertheless not my will, but thine, be done."

In special moments of his life Jesus was thus strengthened by this intimate relationship with God as Father. We need look no further for the explanation of Jesus' astonishing assurance and bravery in the episodes of his life. He was sustained by this inner relationship of union with God as Father. Those nights in prayer on the hillsides must have passed in hours of intimate union with God, Son and Father together, in an intensity which our thoughts cannot hope to penetrate.

What Jesus experienced in prayer he taught to all. For everyone, God was a loving Father, boundlessly compassionate, infinitely understanding. This conviction went against the accepted wisdom of the ancient world. Wisdom in the ancient world was based on evidence and meant pessimism. People looked at the natural world with its unpredictable, uncontrollable forces of destruction—plagues, famines, earthquakes and countless other natural disasters against which they seemed powerless. They also remembered human history—an endless tale of cruelty, exploitation of the weak by the strong, wars, rapacity, despotism, short-lived happiness. Empire succeeded empire and always the rich and powerful prospered at the expense of the poor. In this world of cruel nature and crueller humanity, people passed their short lives. Goodness and justice and mercy were seldom to be found in prominent places. The bad drove out the good.

The wise person accepted this and settled for a cultured, practical pessimism, making the best of a mixed life of good and bad experiences, not expecting too much. The gods were not to be trusted; one had to be wary in dealing with them. Shakespeare summed up this pagan, pre-Christian attitude in *King Lear*. The Earl of Gloucester, just after he has had his eyes put out, cried:

> As flies to wanton boys are we to the gods;
> They kill us for their sport.

The forces behind this world were neither to be trusted nor admired. They were cruel and irresponsible.

Jesus proclaimed the opposite. The Deity was not a capricious tyrant. He was a loving Father, occupied with ceaseless concern for his children. He cared for all people, had a providence toward them. The hairs of their heads were numbered in love. Even the sparrows were part of this merciful providence. Every human being was precious to God. As Father he loved each singly. Even when they sinned he still went on loving them and hoping for their return to him. God willed good, not evil, upon all his children. Jesus did not preach this doctrine from a book-lined study. He preached it from the marketplace. He was, as we have seen, acquainted with the worst evils and ills that befell his contemporaries. In that situation, to that audience, he maintained that God loved them with a fatherly love. Jesus was an optimist and had faith. You need faith to be able to say that God is good and caring to people who have suffered in life. An afternoon in a cancer ward, or the funeral of a child run over going to school, is often enough to stretch faith to its limits. Jesus passed his days among the sick and the oppressed and still said that God was a loving Father. His faith was so great that it communicated itself to the suffering crowds. They too began to believe in the goodness of God, that it was possible they could be lifted out of their misery and be healed. That was how God began to reign among the people: the kingdom of God was there.

Jesus practiced what he preached. It was evident that he really believed what he said about God being a loving Father, for he lived a life of prayer and poverty of spirit. He cast his cares upon his Father and so lived without anxiety about "life, what he was to eat or what he was to drink, his body, what to put on." Usually a person's detachment from anxieties is the best sermon he can preach; joy and serenity, which come from prayer, speak louder than words. This must certainly have been so with Jesus. What gave his words their remarkable authority was his witness of poverty and his life of prayer. It was obvious that his relationship with God as Abba was the most real thing in his life. People therefore sat up and listened when he told them to seek first God's kingdom and his righteousness. He made them want to do the same. When sufficient numbers showed signs of being affected by this teaching then the reign of God was beginning to grow. Unfortunately both signs of the kingdom, limitless love of human beings beyond the Law's taboos and limitless love of the Father wider than Temple worship, were the very things which disturbed the authorities at Jerusalem. Opposition to Jesus began to mount and plans were set in motion which began the process which brought Jesus to his eventual death at Calvary. Thus the sign of the reign of God which was to redeem humankind became not a sign of success and triumph, but the sign of the cross. Redemption came to humankind, but by the blood of the Redeemer.

FOUR

Redemption

The flight of the apostles from the garden when Jesus was arrested was perhaps not cowardice so much as the realization that Jesus did not have God on his side, for according to their beliefs failure meant that God was not with him. They fled because they thought that God had deserted Jesus. (Later, on the cross, Jesus had the same dreadful thought.) The resurrection of Jesus from the dead transformed the scene for those who believed in him. It convinced them that God was indeed on Jesus' side. God had vindicated Jesus when it seemed that he had deserted him. Meeting the risen and alive Jesus changed everything. They now realized that God had never deserted Jesus, even in his darkest hour, and that the cross, disaster that it was, was somehow part of a mysterious divine plan. Abruptly they had to alter the conclusions which had begun to form in the wake of the event of Calvary.

One dawning realization was that the old covenant had come to an end and a new one had begun. They must have remembered Jesus' words at the Last Supper about the new covenant in his blood. They began to see how totally new was the kingdom which Jesus proclaimed. As we know, they continued at first to frequent the Temple and presumably still regarded the priests and scribes as valid authorities in religion; but we also know that their preaching soon landed them in trouble with the priests who had Peter and John imprisoned for preaching that Jesus had risen from the dead. The breach between the followers of the old and new dispensations had begun, symbolized in the gospel stories of the veil of the Temple being torn from top to bottom the moment Jesus died.

A more appalling realization was that the Jewish

authorities had put to death the long-awaited Messiah! This must have been an awesome thought for Jews brought up on the scriptures and the national expectation of the Messiah. When the time came the official representatives of God in his Chosen People had actually rejected and killed the Lord's Anointed! This realization lies behind the writing of the gospels, and we know that it caused St. Paul agony of mind (Rom 9). It happened because the Messiah, when he came, came in an unexpected way saying unexpected things. So the New Testament was founded on the unexpected. Two thousand years later it still seems odd that in God's eternal plan the ultimate order of things should be founded on a rejection by the preparatory order of things. To put it another way, God spent hundreds of years preparing his Chosen People for the arrival of the Messiah, who would usher in the final development of God's dealings with the human race, and when that Messiah came, God's Chosen People rejected him. The old establishment had been formed, yet God's plan turned out to be to build the new establishment without recognition from the old. What happened was an abrupt break, not a smooth transition. This should be a surprise to us, as well as a warning about religious establishments. The answer to the surprise is, of course, that God respects human freedom. He does not force human beings against their will even when those human beings acting against him are his official representatives. So when Caiaphas turned against Jesus and had him suppressed, God let it happen; then, out of that disaster God drew our redemption. We only understand the mystery of the cross when we remember that it was a *mistake*. It should not have happened, the Chosen People should have welcomed and listened to their Messiah, even "coming from Nazareth" and "being the friend of sinners"; it was not God's will that he should be killed by the People of God. The cross should not have happened.

A third significant conclusion from the resurrection was one that we take for granted, but the apostles had to learn. Jesus' teaching and inauguration of the kingdom was not just a Jewish affair, but was for all, even for the heretic Samaritans and the pagan Romans and Greeks. The resurrection took Jesus' movement in Israel, which was Jewish through and through, and made it worldwide. The gospels finish with Jesus appearing to his followers after the resurrection and sending them out to the ends of the world to spread his message. They began to see Jesus in a new light, not just as a Galilean figure of importance to the Jews, but as the Son of God who came to do something for the whole human race from the beginning to the end of time. The doctrine of the redemption was born. The kingdom Jesus preached was no longer seen as a religious movement for Israel, but as a new life for all. The importance of Jesus in history was cosmic, not local. Jesus had done something for everyone, not just for his Jewish contemporaries.

How much was the redemption of the human race in the consciousness of Jesus? Did he know that he was redeeming mankind? Surely not in the terms and categories of later theology, or even those about original sin and justification used by St. Paul in the epistle to the Romans. It seems clear, however, in the gospels, that as Jesus saw that his journey to Jerusalem would result in his death he began to identify himself with Isaiah's Suffering Servant by whose wounds many were to be healed. He saw that his death would be his chief work. "For the Son of man also came not to be served but to serve, and to give his life as a ransom for many" (Mk 10:45). Ideas later developed in the New Testament and church teachings are there at least implicitly.

> During his ministry Jesus spent himself on the work of reconciling and liberating sinners. It would seem almost unaccountably odd that the vicarious value of his impending death never occurred to him. Once he came to expect a violent death, how could he have failed to be concerned with its atoning power?[1]

1. Gerald O'Collins, *The Calvary Christ* (Philadelphia: Westminster Press, 1977).

The first thing that Jesus did for his contemporaries, and therefore for all men and women, was to give them an inspiring example. That is the first way of understanding the redemption: a new way of life taught by words and deeds. It was a revelation from God on how to live. As we saw in the last chapter, the fount of revelation was the person of Jesus himself. He produced words and deeds which have never been forgotten. There was Jesus' faith in the Father which he maintained against all the evidence even after his disciples had wavered and fled from Gethsemane. Some of his agony on the cross must have come from being a public spectacle of abandonment by God. For three years he had put new heart into people by promising them that God was a Father who cared for them individually. On the cross he appeared to have been wrong about that, a ridiculous sight, a false prophet. This was surely why he cried out that he had been deserted by God. Perhaps he himself wavered and thought his life had been a complete mistake, that he had been wrong about God. Most of the bystanders would have agreed. But we know his faith rallied before the end. In St. Luke's gospel Jesus dies renewing his faith in the Father: "Father, into thy hands I commit my spirit." A notable contribution of Christianity to religious thought has been the conviction that human failure does not necessarily mean abandonment by God, but can even mean God's approval. This is a reversal of Old Testament thinking about evil and poverty. In the Old Testament people see suffering and poverty and wonder what sins have been committed. In the New Testament suffering has nothing to do with personal sin. It can be a sign of a good life, even a sign of God's special love. In the New Testament prosperity is likely to be the result of sin, not of virtue. The truth that we have been redeemed by the cross of Jesus, by his failure not his success, is a religious revelation of outstanding importance. The instrument God used to reveal this was the human faith of Jesus in his passion. He died having faith that the failure of his movement and his appalling suffering was a way to God's heart, the way to fulfil his mission, not evidence that God was displeased. In the resurrection God the Father gloriously vindicated this belief.

The second revelation of Jesus was his love. Occasionally we meet people who appear to have set no bounds to Christian love in their daily life. They have abandoned common sense in favor of helping their neighbor far beyond what is sensible and wise: not a few people helped, but a limitless number; not an hour's patient waiting, but a whole afternoon; not a night out of bed with a person in need, but night after night. At first people like this frighten us; the limitlessness of their love stretches our mind. But later we are encouraged and inspired by them because they show what can be done. Their imagination has vaulted upward and expanded the possibilities of Christian love. I think, perhaps, that the limitlessness of Jesus' love for others was what caught the imagination of his contemporaries. He set no bounds, broke even consecrated barriers, in his love for his neighbors, friends and enemies alike. This, too, has been part of the redemption: a revelation of the possibilities open to us to become involved in helping our fellow human beings, including the frightening possibility that there is no limit to how far we should and can go.

Some today would say that when we have spoken about Christ's inspiring teaching and example and shown how he revealed a new way of life to us, leaving the world immeasurably richer by what he said and did, we have said the essential truth about redemption. The impact of Jesus' integrity on the world was his saving work. Such people stop short at theories of atonement whereby Jesus is said to have altered the relationship between humanity and God by his death, "redeeming man by his blood." But to leave out the aspect of atonement is to dismiss much of what the first generations of Christians, who were close to Christ, understood about his death. Epistles, gospels and Apocalypse all have a strong sense that Jesus affected the relationship between humankind and God by more than example and teaching. They hold that Jesus' death and resurrection atoned for our sins and united us to God. The fact that the Christian church has held to this belief for two thousand years is a strong reason for continuing to hold it today. I do not believe that our century, for all its scholarship, is necessarily more perceptive about the work that Jesus performed in the world than his first followers were.

Jesus almost certainly saw his death as a completion of his work, a "ransom for many." Amidst all the pain and fear he offered his death on the cross to complete his life's task of inaugurating the kingdom. He regarded his death as fruitful for many. Our acceptance of this as true depends on our believing Jesus to be our representative before God. The belief makes sense if we hold that on the cross Jesus was representing all of us. If he were just a lone individual, then his death is only valuable as a striking accompaniment to his teaching. If, however, he was our representative before God, then his offering on the cross represents us before God and unites us to God because we can presume that God has found the offering acceptable. It is precisely this idea of one man representing all human beings before God which 20th-century Western men and women find difficult. It sounds primitive to us. *How can my individual cause be pleaded by another? Is it ethically possible for his act of reconciliation with the Father to be efficacious for me? Does this not turn God into a touchy schoolmaster who has to be approached by his favorite pupil before he is pleased with the whole class? Surely Jesus himself insisted on everyone being able to approach God in trust personally? Why the need for a redeemer to put me right with God? Can I not do it myself by saying I am sorry for my sins and loving God directly?*

The answers lie in the phrase *both-and,* both Jesus and me. I am not personally reconciled to the Father by Jesus if I do not cooperate, if I do not also confess my sins and love God. Jesus' reconciling death does not work reconciliation for me if I do not also join in the same reconciling act. Nor does Jesus' inspiring teaching save me unless I accept the teaching and try to live by it. His teaching by itself will not make me better. In other words, Jesus' reconciling work for us all is as a representative, not as a substitute. His offering of his life to the Father is not a substitute for our doing so, but rather it is the first act which enables us and sustains us all in following suit. Once Jesus inaugurated his kingdom on the cross, all his followers can be redeemed in the kingdom by him and alongside him. He represents us before God and then we follow and do the same "in him." I think we have to recognize that Western men and women, after four hundred years of individualism, have lost the sense of solidarity among human beings which allows us to think in terms of a representative person. People from Africa or Asia do not find the same difficulty and can more easily understand that Christ's act is redemptive for them. Tribal people especially preserve a solidarity of thought and action which we have lost since the Renaissance. If we were to get this sense back, we could understand this deeper communal aspect of Jesus' death on the cross with more ease. In addition, when we consider, as we shall in the next chapter, that Jesus was God-made-man, it helps us understand even better why he can be representative of us all. Understanding Jesus as our representative makes us not only glad of what Jesus did on Calvary but also proud. There, in the history of the passion and death, is humanity at its best, in the person of Jesus, being faithful to the highest ideal of love. We can be proud and thankful that "we" did so well on Calvary. The Father, in turn, was proud and thankful for "our" fidelity to him when Jesus said, "It is finished." One of the sentiments that we could have as we kneel before a crucifix is solidarity with Jesus in his achievement. This, as we shall see, was a key idea for St. Paul.

I accept the idea of redemption by Jesus' atoning death as an enriching element of my relationship with him. His death saved me, put me right with God, introduced me to the kingdom of grace, opened up the possibility of a life of union here and now with the Godhead. For this I am eternally thankful. It is the core of my Christian life. This does not mean, however, that I subscribe to a concept of atonement

which says that God was angry, wrathful with Jesus on ac-
count of humanity's sins, and willed the sufferings of Jesus on
the cross as an appeasement to his divine anger. The spiritual
ideas that center around this set of theories are gruesome and
untrue. The teaching that Jesus gave about God throughout
his public life is of the compassionate, loving Father—the
Father of the Prodigal Son. We cannot, in view of that, try to
explain Jesus' death in terms of a God punishing Jesus
because of someone else's sins, taking it out on his Son
because of us. That picture of God is grotesquely out of keeping with the gospel revelation. It is a sad commentary on people's failure to understand the gospel message that it should
ever have been accepted as an explanation of what is meant
by Jesus' atonement for our sins. He atoned for our sins by
pleasing God by the offering of his life, passion and death;
but God was waiting to be pleased, expectant with love, not
sulking in hurt anger. So if, in simple fashion, we ask what
the Father was doing during the passion of Jesus, the answer
is that he was neither punishing Jesus in wrath, nor abandon-
ing him to desolation on the cross, but all the time supporting
him in love. Where was God and what was he doing at
Calvary? ". . . in Christ God was reconciling the world to
himself, not counting their trespasses against them" (2 Cor
5:19).

Once we understand that God truly is a Father who
loves us all, we are able to understand the place of the cross in
the history of redemption. The pain, the blood, the torture,
the fears of Jesus in his passion—were they necessary? Did
God the Father will them? In one sense, yes; in a deeper
sense, no. The cross was necessary in the sense that Jesus had
to go through with it once he was threatened with it. He
could not withdraw. He had to be faithful to his mission by
taking his message to Jerusalem. Going to Jerusalem meant
that he would be arrested and subjected to the cross; he
prophesied that. Insofar as going to Jerusalem was necessary
for Jesus, then, the cross was necessary for him, as he said to

the two disciples at Emmaus. Since the cross was a necessary part of his mission to found the kingdom of God, we can say that the cross was a necessary part of the redemption. Without it, in that sense, we would not have been redeemed.

In the deepest possible sense, however, the cross was not God the Father's will. In an intermediate sense, given original sin, it was. He did not positively will it, but as with all the evil and pain in this world which comes from what we call original sin, he permitted it. Jesus only suffered because Caiaphas and the council made him suffer. They did that because, like us, they were sinners. It was not, absolutely speaking, inevitable. Only sin made it so. Without sin they would have welcomed him as Messiah with open arms. In that case the kingdom would have been founded without the cross. This means that the cross of Calvary was only necessary because of sin. It was an example, a supreme example, of the power of God and the problem of sinful humanity's freedom. God allows us to do wrong and to cause pain rather than take away our freedom; out of the ensuing disaster God often draws a greater unforeseen good with the result that in the end we are glad the original wrong and pain took place. We are able to say when all is over: Thank God for the sin which brought forth such virtue. That happens all the time—a person comes closer to God after sinning, a marriage heals because it has nearly come apart, tension in a family produces striking virtue out of disaster and panic. What we call the cross in our lives is more often than not the agent of a spiritual growth whose magnitude we could not have expected or planned. So it was with the historic cross on Calvary. God did not will his Son to suffer, but once it became inevitable, he allowed it to happen in order that it should become the source of untold graces for the human race. When, therefore, we sing that God "sent his Son to die," we must understand that God sent his Son to inaugurate his kingdom among us and that, inevitably and regrettably, this meant sending his Son to die, human beings being what they are, sin being a fact. Unless we understand this *regret* in God, we run the risk of picturing the Father as taking pleasure in the tortures of Calvary or, worse still, of planning them.

FIVE:

Seek
First
the Kingdom

In this 20th century, Christians say simply that Jesus is God. It is worth recalling that it took some time for the first Christians to come to such an explicit statement. There was a gradual approach, first through more long-winded phrases in the epistles, then to the use of the word *is* in St. John's gospel at the end of the New Testament era. The epistles use phrases like "Jesus, whom God made our wisdom, our righteousness and sanctification and redemption" (1 Cor 1:30); "He reflects the glory of God and bears the very stamp of his nature" (Heb 1:3); "He is the image of the invisible God" (Col 1:15); "Jesus . . . did not count equality with God a thing to be grasped" (Phil 2:6). These are rich, impressive statements, especially when taken in the context in which each of them is used. But none of them is yet quite so blunt as to state that Jesus is God. It is only in the prologue of St. John's gospel, which belongs to the end of the first century and to the latest New Testament writing, that Christians progressed to the simple statement: ". . . the Word was God . . . and the Word became flesh."

There is nothing suspect about this slow progress. It is, in fact, how we all proceed when faced with an important event or significant person. We take time to discover all the aspects of the subject and, as we go along, new ideas and insights strike us which were dormant till then. We see a facet of the situation we never saw before; a new train of thought is opened up; a new interim conclusion is reached. Finally

the whole person, or event, comes together in our mind, and
we see with simplicity the integral truth. I have noticed that
my ideas about people I meet take time to mature, so that my
final judgment of them is on the one hand the same as earlier
judgments but on the other hand much richer and
deeper—and truer. This last judgment is also simpler, able to
be expressed in *is*, not needing to be hedged about with
longer phrases and *mights* and *coulds*. For instance, a social
worker just getting to know a client will venture an interim
judgment: "Robert appears to manifest a dependence on
alcohol." This sort of cautious statement is all she can in
honesty manage. But a member of Robert's family who has
lived with him and loves him will say, "Bob is a drunkard."
The longer acquaintance and the closer love make the word *is*
possible.

I suggest that that is how the first members of the church
progressed in their knowledge of Jesus. Those who had been
with him had experienced the divine in him: his matchless
authority; the high demands he made upon people (as from
God); the peculiar closeness to God and the manner in which
he spoke of his Father; the way he healed and forgave sins;
his whole manner of being both completely a man and also
intangibly something more. He acted as if he were God, but
none of them would have said he was God. They needed
more time for that. They knew him to be Son of God, a
special, nay, unique, revelation of God to their time. Clearly
he bore the very stamp of God's nature, was a visible image
of invisible Yahweh. His work was divine; God was with him
in all he did. After the resurrection they prayed to him. So,
long before St. John put it simply and succinctly in his prologue, they were for practical purposes regarding Jesus as
God incarnate. The prologue of St. John merely expressed in
words what they were believing in their hearts.

The implications of the incarnation are as mind-
stretching as the event. Perhaps those of us who accept the incarnation easily could learn from those who do not accept it.
Some do not accept it because the implications are too im-

possible: God put to death by his creatures; God a criminal; God flogged by Roman soldiers; God a man. We who believe in the incarnation could well start at that end of the truth, the implications; then, only if we can accept them, ought we proceed to believing in the fact that Jesus Christ was God. We can, in other words, learn not to be too glib about Jesus being God from those who cannot believe it.

The implications of Jesus' life can best be approached by the consideration that in the history of the human race God became human only once. It is therefore important to see what sort of person he became. It is legitimate to suppose that the divine choice of what kind of human life to live would be "on purpose" and not accidental. The life of God-as-man has to be seen as a commentary from God on human excellence. In becoming human, God is saying: *That is the kind of human life I want you to imitate; those are values I want you to have; when you have children, bring them up to aim at the things Jesus aimed at, for those aims are what human excellence consists in; do not be led into thinking that other aims are more worthwhile.* When, however, we examine the life of Jesus we are in for a shock, because we find that Jesus' life and ambitions simply do not match the average ambitions of a modern person. Jürgen Moltmann sums this up well when he says, "God did not become man according to the measure of our concept of being a man. He became the kind of man we do not want to be: an outcast, accursed, crucified."[1]

We could make a list of the things that most of us want to be and want our children to be, and then we could make a list of the things that Jesus of Nazareth was during his life. The two lists would be startlingly different. The first list might include: owning property, having a settled job, having financial security, having a happy marriage and family, being approved of by society, moving upwards socially, securing a job in the professions, not upsetting the community we

1. Jürgen Moltmann, *The Crucified God* (New York: Harper and Row, 1974).

live in, retiring with the approval of our peers, keeping in with the church. It is fair to say that these are probably what most schools aim to prepare their pupils for, including Christian schools. If we next compare that list of worthy aims against the life of Jesus, God-made-man, we find a big difference. Jesus was apparently not property-owning and lived without the need for it; Jesus, during his public ministry, had no settled job but was itinerant; Jesus had no financial security and told his followers not to bother about it; Jesus upset the community he lived in—even his family was against him; he did not retire with honor or approval but was done away with by the religious leaders of his community; and his death between two criminals on Calvary was certainly not a socially upward move. As Moltmann said, Jesus chose to be the sort of man we do not choose to be. This makes it challenging for us to pursue the imitation of Christ.

There is no easy answer to this problem. Some of the things that God incarnate chose to be were because of his special mission to be a prophet—the itinerant life and no marriage, for instance. We can presume that those aspects of Jesus' life belong to his peculiar vocation and are not for general imitation. God does not want us all to be itinerant and not to marry. Settled life, marriage, security, are part of the blessings of creation; they make for Christian peace and harmony. On the other hand we are not entitled to use the special vocation argument indiscriminately with regard to Jesus' life. We cannot dismiss all he did as so unique that we cannot be expected to try to imitate him. There must be some aims of Jesus which were deliberately chosen as lessons in human excellence for us all, and other aims which he no less clearly avoided for the same purpose of showing us how to live—the desire for social approval, for instance, or the aim to make money as the basis for a choice of career. I believe we can solve the dilemma by remembering that for Jesus the main aim was an internal one, seeking his Father's will, and only secondarily was it the external list which we enumerated above. That being said, we must take seriously the historical fact that being obedient to the Father for Jesus did mean poverty, torture and martyrdom. Those things were not accidental to Jesus' life. They were direct results of doing God's will. We should not expect to be let off any more lightly. The life chosen by God-become-man is not for slavish imitation from the outside: Jesus was poor, so I must be poor; Jesus was hated, so I must be hated. However, the life of Christ is for imitation, imitation in its deepest, and most challenging, essential: the pursuit of God's reign totally and without regard for other ambitions.

The one pursuit of Jesus was to seek first the kingdom and the values of the kingdom. This was his life's ambition, given him at his baptism, and worked out that month in the desert which followed his anointing by the Spirit. He neither aimed for poverty nor riches, for approval or disapproval, for a movement socially up or down. His eyes were not fixed on those intermediate and relative goals—his eyes were fixed on inaugurating the kingdom. Everything was judged in the light of that; his treasure was in that, so his heart was there too. The lesson, then, that Jesus' life gives us is not to make intermediate aims like the choices of poverty or riches, approval or disapproval, important. Seek first the kingdom. Everything else then, in fact, follows—or not, as the case may be. I would say that the education in human excellence which the incarnation offers us is to be clear that the first aim in life is citizenship in the kingdom of God (limitless love for one another, complete trust in Abba, our God). Christian education has to make its full commitment to that and see security, settled job, financial success, harmonious home life, approval by society, for what they are—secondary, not necessary, aims of life. Seek first the kingdom is the lesson of the cross. Another way of putting this is to say that love is the only Christian absolute, all else is relative.

Christianity for us must not be a question of living in society, accepting the standards and ideals of that society, and then adding a Christian layer to our life as top-dressing. It seems so easy to do that: to accept that the way of life of the

West, with its attendant customs, the class system, international exploitation, military overspending, snobbery, waste,
personal affluence, is the life we have to live, to which in all
sincerity we then add our Christian portion of Mass-going,
parish support, devoted personal charity and prayer. To do
this is to accept the world as arbiter of our way of life
alongside Jesus Christ. But Christians are commanded to
make Jesus Christ their sole arbiter of morals, not to give him
a place as one of several arbiters. In other words, the imitation and following of Christ is meant to be for his followers
the whole of the cake of life, not just the icing on the top.
Karl Rahner in a prayer to God the Father says:

> Man finds you only where you choose to be found . . .
> everyman's road to eternal life, even though it leads to
> your infinity which is everywhere, must still take the
> detour through that definite human being who was
> born in Palestine under Emperor Augustus and died
> under the Governor Pontius Pilate. . . . Your grace
> comes to us not in the always and everywhere of your
> all-pervasive Spirit, but in the here and now of Jesus
> Christ.

When we divide our interests and accept our moral aims un-
critically from society while looking to our religious tradition
for help in prayer and devotion we are not making that
necessary detour through Jesus of Nazareth that Rahner
speaks of. We are not taking Christ with the seriousness he
expects of his followers. We are accepting division into our
life, accepting social standards from one direction (non-
Christian) and religious standards from another (Christ). A
remark of St. Ignatius of Antioch is apposite: "Do not have
Jesus Christ on your lips and the world in your hearts."

The institutional church is often little help in this matter. Historically the church has been sometimes eager to
make friends with the world, ready to dilute the absoluteness
of Christ's command to seek first the kingdom in the interests
of a working compromise in order to help its flock. It is

arguable that this tradition of supping with the Devil is pastorally wise and pays in the long run. But it is also arguable that there is a loss of witness to Christ's gospel and a perceptible lowering of spiritual temperature when this is done. As President Julius Nyerere of Tanzania pointed out:

> Certainly the Church has traditionally found little difficulty in operating in capitalist states, even when those were highly autocratic or totalitarian. It adapts to the government pattern, operating within it, and does welfare work among the losers in the economic game. In very recent years, individuals (even bishops) in some Latin American countries have begun to recognize that this is not enough; but even now the Church as an institution does not—as far as I know—hold anxious seminars about its role in such conditions.[2]

At the local level some Catholic organizations bear within themselves this compromise over standards. They come together in all zeal for a spiritual purpose and set themselves a spiritual program, but simultaneously they bring into their organizations ideas which have little to do with the gospel and could even be against it, like class or money qualifications. In doing this they adulterate their following of Jesus and to that extent fall short in his discipleship. Once I was asked to speak to a Catholic organization which has "good birth" as one of its entry qualifications. We met in one of the city's top hotels which by chance was situated a few hundred yards from the slums where I once worked as a priest. I was asked to speak on the "Universal Vocation to Sanctity" and I suggested that the members' call to sanctity had plenty to do with those slum dwellers down the road, who could not be ignored and who might come up on the agenda of the Last Judgment of those present. The audience was very polite to me, but frankly not interested. Most of them were landowners who probably exercised justice and charity to a high degree on their estates.

2. Julius Nyerere, *The Tablet*, March 31, 1981.

The city was for them a place of work or entertainment, but otherwise distasteful, so they could not be expected to be interested in slums. It was clear that they ignored them. (Those were the days before urban riots.) Their class narrowness prevented them from thinking in gospel terms about their slum-dwelling brothers and sisters in the city.

It is easy to fire off criticisms from the outside of organizations, but I am certain that when a Christian society brings in worldly standards to that extent, it positively hinders Christ's work because it ignores the implications of the incarnation of God in the man from Bethlehem, Nazareth and Capernaum. Those implications are stark; nothing less than the obligation to take the life of Jesus of Nazareth as normative in whatever circumstances we find ourselves, "To take the detour through that definite human being who was born in Palestine." Both individuals and (especially) the church, which defends the doctrine, have to prove that they believe that Jesus Christ was God incarnate by living as if it were true. This is not adequately done by merely stating the truth verbally. The verbal truth has to be accompanied by an attempt to imitate Christ in the way he lived, because his style of life was not an accident but a divine commentary on how to live as a human being. If we become Christians whose manner of living is governed by worldly principles of social prestige or money and not by Christ's life, people are entitled to wonder whether we really believe that Jesus Christ was God-made-man, and that his life was the Word for all men and women on how to live.

PART TWO:

Our Work

SIX:

The
Christian
Life

Discipleship in Christ

One way of assessing the value of Jesus Christ's life and death is to ask ourselves what life would be like had Jesus never lived. Leaving aside the impact Jesus had upon world history, what would our personal lives be if Jesus had not been born? To begin with, we would not have the specific teaching we call the gospel to live by. Merely to imagine that is to feel naked. Our life would be without a yardstick to measure conduct by, without an "impossible" ideal to pursue; we would have nothing to aim at, or fall short of. No Sermon on the Mount, no parables, Good Samaritan, Prodigal Son. . . . We take Jesus' teaching for granted so often that it is salutary to imagine what it would be like to have no such ideals placed before us, and no Christian story to hand on to the next generation. Alongside the loss of Jesus' teaching, we would also be deprived of his wonderful example. We would have no gospel stories to tell one another, no crucifixes and pictures of Calvary to hang in our churches and homes. Lastly, as we saw in Chapter 4, no Jesus Christ would mean no access to the Father, no strengthening in the Holy Spirit for our Christian lives, no Jesus in heaven pleading our cause as a powerful advocate before the Father. It is difficult to put into words, but living in the 20th century without Christianity and the life of Jesus in the first century would be an empty and dismal affair. Those foundation events of our religion are nearer to our heart than we think.

We saw in Chapter 4 that redemption takes place in two steps. The first stage is what Jesus did. The second stage is what a person does to assimilate into his or her life that first stage. The whole of Jesus' teaching, and his redemptive work on the cross, is of no avail to us unless we decide to accept that teaching, to embrace that redemptive work. The second part of this book is about our second stage. It is about our discipleship of Christ, how we align ourselves with him and become his followers. Although free agents with regard to choosing Christ, we are not, of course, alone and powerless for one moment. We have the Holy Spirit, God himself as spiritual energy and love, in our hearts to help us be Christians. Jesus described his rising from the dead as going back to the Father so as to be able to send the Spirit upon his followers. Pentecost and the outpouring of the Spirit on the church was the result. This second stage, then, of Christian discipleship is dominated by the Spirit of God as much as the first was by Jesus, the Son of God. These two manifestations of God's power in the world do not work against each other. The Holy Spirit dwells in the church and in each individual solely to point us to Christ and to carry on Christ's work in us. There is no new work of God, only an inspired deepening of the first work, a continuation in each personal life of the inauguration of the reign of God started by Jesus in history.

What must we do to be followers of Jesus Christ? Jesus himself gave the answer:

> "If any man would come after me, let him deny himself and take up his cross and follow me. For whoever would save his life will lose it; and whoever loses his life for my sake and the gospel's will save it" (Mk 8:34-35).

I suppose the reader like myself must have looked at that passage many times and tried to apply it to his or her life. I have sometimes been baffled by it, because phrases like *losing life* are none too obvious in meaning—does Jesus expect us to

denigrate or underuse our humanity? I have also been
frightened by this passage, as I have begun to discern the
message of being ready to give all which emerges from the
words—no easy, compromise Christianity is allowed. Then,
too, I have been uplifted, because there is something glorious
about being invited to give all for a cause, and in view of
what we have seen about Jesus' mission, to be asked to give
everything "for the gospel's sake" is inspiring. When I
remember, as well, that at the moment he took up his cross
Jesus was frightened and had to draw upon all his resources
of trust in the Father, I am comforted as well as inspired.

A cool look at the words themselves reveals a triple invitation to those who want to be followers of Christ. We are
to deny ourselves, to take up our cross, and to lose our lives. I
do not think we need try to spot a progression here. More to
the point is to take the phrases as one challenging call. At first
it looks negative: deny self, bear cross, lose life. There is no
description of the positive benefits which come to those who
perform this negative thing. On reflection that is the point.
The Christian is not invited to follow Christ on a bargain
basis, to give up this good in order to get that greater good.
There is no appeal to higher self-interest. There is just the appeal to give up everything because of Jesus Christ and his
gospel. The call is a call for a step into the unknown; the
things we will suffer, the dreadful losses, are outlined, but
the good we receive at the end of the step is only mentioned
as saving life. We have to take what that means in faith. The
call is a call to faith, to be faithful to Jesus Christ. Personal
invitations like that do not operate on an If-you-come-I-will-
give-you-rewards basis. That is not the language of love. The
language of love is: Come and see; trust me; follow me; stay
with me. All through the ages the saints have done that. They
have not calculated the loss and gain in following Jesus. They
have just answered the call, and each day grown deeper and
deeper into discipleship. They have let go.

In the business of letting go we have externally the
memory of Jesus' passion and death to help us. Internally we

have more than a memory. We have the presence of the Holy Spirit. Our Christian work is really the Spirit's Christian work, for that is why the Spirit is there and what he does. We let go in order to allow the Spirit to take over. St. Paul made much of this internal work of redemption in the Christian. He seldom used the phrase "redeemed by Christ"; he liked to say "redeemed in Christ." Redeemed by Christ implies a gap between Christ and us, the gap of centuries between A.D. 30 and now. Jesus died and rose years ago; we are redeemed now. St. Paul's phrase, however, abolishes that time gap. We are redeemed in Christ. Christ's act of redemption and our redemption are going on together. There is a mystical union between us. Time is abolished. This can mean two things, and St. Paul said them both. It can mean that Christ is with my cross, and that I was with Christ's cross. First, it can mean that the day-to-day work of my discipleship, of my being redeemed and redeeming the world, is here and now suffused with the presence of the crucified Christ: Christ's death and life are, now, present in my death and life (for the sake of the gospel). Second, being redeemed in Christ can mean that when Christ died and rose, then, on Calvary, in some mysterious way, annihilating time, I was there too: My being a Christian places me on the cross with Christ. St. Paul said both these things when he was talking about the life of the baptized Christian:

> Do you not know that all of us who have been baptized into Christ Jesus were baptized into his death? We were buried therefore with him by baptism into death, so that as Christ was raised from the dead by the glory of the Father, we too might walk in newness of life (Rom 6:3-4).

These words are mysterious, but they undoubtedly mean that baptism creates a union between the Christian and the crucified Christ which is internal and across time. Christianity is not just following a figure who lived in history. It involves an internal transformation by the living Spirit of that same figure. Christianity has a mystical dimension. Taking up the cross to follow Christ is not, therefore, only an external following of that figure in history in the light of all we know about him. It is chiefly a letting go inside ourselves in order to be united to that powerful redeemer in the here and now of our daily living. Letting go is a personal surrender to Christ, now, in each of us. This second stage of redemption is personal surrender. It is by turns frightening and comforting, as every reader will know. It is always worth it. "For what does it profit a man, to gain the whole world and forfeit his life?" (Mk 8:36).

In St. John's gospel Jesus uses the striking example of the vine and the branches to explain this continuing union of redemption between us and himself. Vine and branches are one; it is not easy to spot a distinction between parent stem and branches in the vine bush—the plant is all branches, or all trunk, depending on how you look at it. The vine produces grapes *at the end of the branches*. The sap from the trunk rises to spread through the whole bush as far as the branch ends where the grapes grow. The effort to produce grapes is a joint one of trunk and branches. So it is with Christ and us. When Jesus returned to the Father he left his followers behind to go on doing what he had been doing. His followers were to *be him* in the world. He would be present and bear fruit in them. They would do what he had been doing, spreading the reign of God to all who would accept it. The union between Jesus and his followers was so close that he simply described their presence in the world as his presence: "I am with you always, to the close of the age."

In his ministry in Palestine Jesus went about healing people, caring for them, listening to them, teaching. He asks his followers to carry on the work, and promises that when they do, it will be he doing so. His followers, then, are Jesus' eyes, ears, tongue, hands and caring heart in the world today. They act; he acts. That is what the church is: vine and branches together producing fruit. But we are free—free to say yes and cooperate, free to say no and refuse. When we say yes it is an exciting thought that it is not just ourselves but Christ who is doing the action, speaking through us, inspiring us with his words, supporting our feeble efforts to care for someone with his caring heart. This mystical union with Jesus Christ is, in other words, not only a union of being but also a union of action. Baptism enables us to let go into Christ in a partnership of acting as well as being.

It is, however, an awesome thought that we are free to refuse to cooperate with Christ in the redemptive partnership. We can say no through laziness, or diffidence, or lack of imagination, or any of the numerous reasons for which we human beings are wont to let opportunities pass by. When this happens we stifle the action of Christ, and there is no normal way he makes up for it. Daft as we may think this way of doing things is, it is how Jesus Christ planned his church: Miracles apart, he acts through human beings or not at all. So if I pass by a needy person when I should stop, I have made Christ pass by that needy person. If I stay silent when I should speak out, I have silenced Christ. That we often do this is one of the sadnesses of being Christ's disciple. Once, I arrived at the station to catch the late night train to Edinburgh. Being tired I was glad to find an empty compartment and was just about to stretch myself full length for sleep when, as the train drew out, a young woman breathlessly got in. She slumped in the corner, looking miserably unhappy, saw she was with a priest and said, "I'm fed up with life." My heart sank as I saw a night of lengthy listening looming ahead instead of sleep. So, after only 10 minutes I made an excuse and went to sleep. I pretended to myself that I would help her better in the morning as we bowled through the Scottish lowlands, refreshed by sleep. But, while I was asleep, she got out. She was a West Indian girl. Perhaps she had not been in the country long and had never before been in a situation like that with a sympathetic person. The whole interview could have been set up by God for helping the girl in ideal circumstances. In Christ I could have let go, calmly allowed him to work through me, gently drawn the girl out and let her speak. The sacrifice of my comfort would have helped me to be a keen listener. But I did not let go into Christ. I put myself first and suppressed Christ in me. By my selfishness I made Christ inoperative; the girl may never again meet him so conveniently. The incident, of which I am ashamed, brought home to me the mystery of the baptismal union between Christ and his disciples better than my successes. Christ leaves us free, both to fail by our sins and to succeed by his grace.

PRAYER IN CHRIST

Another union with Jesus Christ, vine and branches together, is that of prayer. We saw that the underlying experience of Jesus in prayer was the relationship of Son to Father, Son to Abba. The redemptive union of the Christian with Christ means nothing less than that that experience is open to each one of us. By baptism we have the Spirit within us whose work is to pray in us the prayer of "Abba." There is a passage in the epistle to the Romans where St. Paul beautifully describes prayer as the provision in our souls of an arena for the Spirit to pray to the Father (Rom 8:26-27). This is Christian prayer at its best. The task for each individual is to realize this, to let go sufficiently in himself or herself to allow this experience to happen. So often in prayer we picture what we are trying to do as a search for God, an attempt to capture him, a reaching out beyond ourselves, some sort of stretching out toward a faraway God. This is an incorrect picture. If we got the picture right in our minds it might help us to pray better. The correct picture is that we are one in our depths with Christ, branches of his vine; he ceaselessly now enjoys communion with the Father, "seated at the right hand of the Father, always making intercession for us." That is going on now, and by our union with Christ, and the Holy Spirit dwelling in our souls, we can join in that heavenly communication both while we are at work and, most especially, when we are at prayer. All it needs is a journey inwards.

It is wrong to think that prayer will always be a felt experience of this divine indwelling. When we pray we probably have more dull experiences than interesting ones. In prayer we can be bored, terribly distracted, fidgety, desperately anxious, obsessed with jealousy. In fact, we are probably more bothered with these sorts of emotions while we pray than at other times; just because we are not occupied with anything else, our surface mind is vulnerable to every passing fancy. Nevertheless, at another level we can be absorbed in union with Christ all the time we pray, and be taken up into his communion with the Father, even while we are distracted on the surface. The art is to be able to descend to this lower level as easily as possible, and this is done not by some special technique but by a gentle letting go. The use of techniques is inappropriate because it can make us tense and leave no room for the Spirit to take over. Techniques in prayer, even of passivity, belong to the realm of activism. In prayer we descend to the level of contact with the indwelling Spirit only by resolute passivity. The only technique worth learning is to go beyond techniques to utter receptivity to God. If we persevere we are sometimes rewarded with that precious experience when fidgety surface and calm interior become one, and the surface of the mind coalesces with the fundamental tranquillity which has welled up from below:

> And the lotus rose, quietly, quietly,
> The surface glittered out of heart of light.[1]

But these are gift moments, and their absence is not a sign of God's displeasure. The important thing is to remain tranquil in the depths. There we are united with the redeeming and worshipping Christ.

SUFFERING IN CHRIST—OUR CROSS

Along with action and prayer a third way of being united to the risen Christ is by suffering. The disciples of

1. T. S. Eliot, *Four Quartets* (New York: Harcourt Brace Jovanovich, Inc., 1968).

Jesus soon realized that following him would for them, too, be a way of the cross. Jesus had made this a mark of his discipleship as we saw in Mark 8:34-35. It was no surprise to the early Christians that they soon had to suffer for their following of Christ. They rejoiced that they were considered worthy of it. Since then a grand tradition has grown up of treating suffering as a special way of being united to Christ and through him to the Father. Generations of Christians have faced suffering with the words of St. Paul in their hearts, "I have been crucified with Christ." The thought has given strength and hope to many who have had to face hardship and pain. They unite their sufferings to Jesus on the cross, and that is their prayer. This is a valuable message for hospital patients who often complain that they cannot pray there. It is helpful to explain that their pain and discomfort is their prayer, that they need not force themselves to do anything more than just be "toward God" in pain; that words, formulas, holy thoughts are not needed because not possible. All they need to do is lie there united in their hearts to Jesus, branches and vine together. Seen in this way a hospital is a tangible experience of Pascal's saying, "Christ is in agony until the end of time."

The Catholic tradition has taken and developed the idea of offering up our suffering in union with the crucified Christ one step further by pointing out that such a union is redemptive for the world. Christ originally died to redeem the world. Our deaths in Christ can be made for the same purpose, can be offered up for special intentions within the general intention of Christ to save humankind. This is a precious heritage, very much in evidence among ordinary people. Visiting in the parish we can be taken aback by the holiness we meet, especially the generous attitude of very ordinary people who uncomplainingly accept hardships from life and offer them up for missionaries, priests, the pope, all sorts of people, sick and well, who would be surprised beneficiaries, if they knew! This union of our sufferings redemptively with Christ is, incidentally, one of the purposes and justifications of the enclosed religious orders. They live hidden, humdrum lives at the level of appearance, but in the depths they are in the center of Christian action, offering their sufferings and prayers in union with Christ in his work of redemption. The Carmelite Order makes a special point of this apostolate. St. Thérèse of Lisieux lived and wrote unforgettably on the subject. Since she died her influence outside Carmelite houses has been enormous.

Some modern writers take issue with this broadening of the idea of cross to include not only suffering undergone in the Christian cause but any suffering whatsoever. They point out that the cross for Jesus was the specific punishment he received for the specific things he did to threaten the authorities. It is scarcely legitimate to make it mean all suffering. Howard Yoder writes:

> The cross of Christ was not an inexplicable or chance event, which happened to strike him, like illness or accident. To accept the cross as his destiny, to move towards it and even to provoke it, when he could well have done otherwise, was Jesus' constantly reiterated free choice; and he warns his disciples lest their embarking on the same path be less conscious of its costs. The cross of Calvary was not a difficult family situation, not a frustration of visions of personal fulfilment, a crushing debt or a nagging in-law; it was the political, legally to be expected result of a clash with the powers ruling his society.[2]

Writers like Yoder conclude that the only sufferings Christians can legitimately call their cross are the ones which they bring upon themselves by their Christian stance in public (and perhaps also in private). This narrows down the concept of cross considerably and is a direct challenge to all those who have been accustomed to face personal hardships like illness or disappointment by calling them their cross and offering them up.

2. Howard Yoder, *The Politics of Jesus* (Grand Rapids: Eerdmans, 1972).

The viewpoint has much to commend it. It is undoubtedly biblical. Jesus, surely, did mean by the phrase
"Take up your cross" the direct imitation of himself in his
work of spreading the kingdom of God. The sufferings which
St. Paul underwent, the beatings, scourgings and shipwrecks
which he so proudly enumerated and "gloried in," were not
the ordinary hardships of life but came as the direct result of
his labors in the spread of the gospel. He was taking up the
cross of Christ and that had been the cross of Calvary, the
particular historical result of the stance Jesus took in his society. It was not a generalized thing, but a historical event.
Christians should not lose sight of this fact. When we put
crucifixes on our walls we are reminding ourselves of that
particular historical event. Crucifixes are not general symbols
of suffering but specific reminders of Jesus' bloody end. We
must not be too glib in using the word *cross* for our day-to-
day frustrations. It does not do justice to Jesus' example to
call every mishap a cross.

On the other hand, the Catholic instinct is surely right to
extend the idea of redemptive suffering beyond the particular
to the general. What makes suffering Christian and redemptive is not only its content (suffering in the cause of Christ)
but also its agent (Christ joined to us). From the point of view
of content, perhaps, only sufferings in the direct cause of the
kingdom qualify as crosses. From the point of view of who
suffers, however, all hardship *can be made* Christian and
therefore redemptive by an act of intention of joining
ourselves, branch to vine, to the redeeming Christ. In that
way we can convert, if we try, all hardships which come our
way into the redemptive cross of Christ by an act of prayerful
offering. To do that is to unite our sufferings with Christ at
the primary level of his obedience to the Father. That was
the level, after all, at which he redeemed us.

Both viewpoints, the narrow and the broad, can learn
from each other. The Catholic tradition should learn from
the radical political one that followers of Jesus should not
normally hide their lights under bushels and make no Chris-

tian contribution to society. We are often called to public action in the cause of Christ. When so called we cannot take refuge in private piety and offering up of crosses. For Christians there can be no option for the quiet life using the concept of "redemptive suffering." We must always be ready to be socially involved. The radicals, in turn, can look at traditional Catholics and learn from the mystical purpose which makes us able to discern the presence of God in the most ordinary events, and so to turn all suffering into an act of partnership in the redemptive work of Christ. In this view the whole of Christ's life was redemptive, not only the climax of his public ministry. So, in seeking union with Christ in his hidden life as well as his public life, his followers are recognizing that all Jesus' life was obedience to the Father and part of the overall plan of redemption. Participating in that is what we call the Christian life, or the paschal mystery. Through this mystery the redemption of the world is still going on. Living the paschal mystery is simply to act, pray, and suffer in union with Jesus Christ, offering every moment of our lives, ordinary and extraordinary, for this continuing redemption of the world. It is a comprehensive challenge, and nothing in our lives is apart from it. The next four chapters are a discussion about how we live the paschal mystery in four key areas of modern living: the world village, change in world and church, personal growth, and Christian sharing. What follows is not meant to be an exhaustive survey, merely a discussion of four important issues of modern Christianity in the light of Christ's work. In taking these four areas for discussion, let us not forget that the areas in between belong to Christ also. All our life is Christ's; all therefore can be redemptive.

SEVEN

World
Village

POLITICAL CHRISTIANITY

The most obvious change in the Catholic church in the last twenty years has been the change in liturgy from the formal Latin Mass to the informal, communitarian Mass in the vernacular. A more profound change, however, which has affected all Christian churches, whether they have had to change liturgically or not, has been in the sphere of moral awareness. Here there has been a profound development. Twenty years ago the majority of Christians conceived their Christian responsibility in terms of personal charity to their neighbors. They did not much think about Christian responsibility for the whole of society. The nation was remote and impersonal; it was, perhaps, too big to think about. They accepted society as it came to them, and put their energy into being good neighbors and witnesses to Christ in the places where they lived and worked. For Catholics this was historically understandable, because the religious attitude of accepting the status quo of society and concentrating on survival as Christians within it is the characteristic attitude of immigrants. In Great Britain, for example, most Catholics were immigrants. They had come largely from Ireland, a few from Europe, between 1850 and 1950. It takes some time for immigrants to become psychologically part of their country of adoption. Predominantly the Catholic attitude in England, Scotland and Wales before 1950 was this immigrant one of individual morality and personal piety. While

I cannot speak from experience of the situation in the United States, I would guess that the same conditions prevailed there.

A wider reason for this individualistic Christianity was the four-hundred-year-old trend in European thought toward individualism and away from community thinking. This affected religion as well as other human values. All denominations of Christianity after the Reformation developed this element: a fervent, warm devotion to God the Father and to Jesus his Son with particular concern for personal salvation but little concern for the world and its betterment. The world was often seen in no other terms than as a formidable obstacle to personal holiness to be treated warily or even avoided at all costs. One other group of Catholics in England was affected by this ethos: those who had kept their faith since the Reformation through all the years of persecution and social disability. When emancipation came, this group retained the religious attitude of intense privacy which had saved their faith for them in penal times, even though it was no longer needed. So this group, like the Irish immigrants but for different reasons, also practiced a Christianity which was concerned with private but not public morals. They tended to take their social and political views from their fellow countrymen of the same social class while being different from them in religious belief. A young person brought up in such a family was proud to be different from his or her country neighbors in religion but would have been ashamed to be different in other matters like politics, social ambitions, ways of treating people. Without recognizing it, such people were living their lives in compartments. For both groups religion tended to belong to the private sphere of life and was not expected to influence public matters like the social divisions of the nation or the nation's role in world affairs. These were part of the background of life, against which individuals pursued their personal ambitions, including a fairly intense desire to know God and to pray. They had no notion that loyalty to Jesus Christ might impel them to try to change these given background elements. That would have seemed bizarre in the extreme.

That was thirty years ago, but it already seems a hundred years ago, further away even than the Latin Mass. Sincere Christians now are busily concerned with the national and international society they live in. Justice and peace, the Third World, Amnesty International, the Peace Movement, the role of the Christian in politics, and many similar ideas impinge upon conscience all the time. In and out of church they are discussed by fellow Christians. There is no possibility of keeping religion in a private sphere where no one else may venture. Discipleship of Jesus Christ has "gone public," because discipleship of Jesus Christ is now seen to be a matter not only of personal prayer and private morals, but also of public worship and national-international behavior. We now know that part of our Christian discipleship is to be concerned about social and political conditions all over the world. This means being concerned about the behavior of governments in far-off and near countries, as well as domestic social matters like how the handicapped are provided for or what goes on in our prisons. Morality, in other words, has become communal as well as personal. We are as concerned about how the various communities we belong to behave as we are about our personal lives. We have become busy Christian bodies in society. We feel we are our brother's keeper.

This development in Christian awareness is sometimes called the political dimension of Christianity. This is accurate as long as it is remembered that it has a broader meaning than being concerned about what goes on in the legislature (politics in the narrow sense), and also that it is not a matter of the church being concerned about her own rights in a country (Christian politics in the narrow sense). The church is now concerned about the human rights of everyone in a country. The church was concerned about her own rights in the world all through the ages of individualism since the Renaissance. She negotiated with kings and made concordats to create religious space for her children. What is newer is a concern by the church to defend human rights in the world quite apart from her own position in any country. The longest document produced by the bishops in the Vatican Council, *The Church in the Modern World*, left behind purely domestic matters and tackled matters of universal human concern. It was not only the longest document, but also the one that broke the newest ground. It was seen at the time as an important breakthrough for a church council to pronounce upon such topics. It has worked as a most effective incentive to the new direction of Catholic Christian awareness ever since.

Not every Catholic is happy about the direction which Christian discipleship has taken. Here is one reaction:

> The Church's business is the relationship of the individual to God. She isn't there to change society but to change people—or rather, to show them, with the help of grace, how to change themselves.[1]

This remark was followed by a lively correspondence between those who agreed and those who disagreed, those who concentrated upon the private aspect of morals and those who championed the public aspect. I do not agree with John Braine because I do not think it possible for the "changed" Christian to stop short at private morality and not to want to change society in accordance with Christian values, but I guess that behind his remark is an accurate perception about two dangers for the modern Christian. The first danger is that we may become so concerned about world politics and the evils being perpetrated in, say, South America, South Africa or Russia, that we may have no eye for our own personal shortcomings, and even allow ourselves to become personally immoral while working for international morality. A subsidiary danger to this is the one of becoming talkers rather than doers. There is not much we can in fact do about evils over the sea, except talk about them. That is dangerous for

1. John Braine, *The Universe*, April 3, 1981.

disciples of Christ, for they may end up talking endlessly about the motes in the eyes of foreign rulers and do nothing about the beams in their own eyes. From my days as university chaplain I remember a student whose Catholicism was of an old-fashioned kind and who had the misfortune to have a room next door to a modern Christian whose room was frequented day and night by students discussing the iniquities of capitalism, multinational commerce and American actions in Vietnam. The noise from that room was unbearable, and my friend got little sleep because of the vociferousness of the Christian concern going on next door. She was learning the hard way, at the receiving end, that people whose Christianity is all talk and programs have a long way to go before being fully Christians, and that in Christianity an ounce of action is worth a ton of political talk.

The second danger of the politically aware Christian is that of making judgments with insufficient and even inaccurate information. When something is wrong in the community I live in, I can go and examine it for myself. All I need do is then make up my mind what needs to be done and do it. Whether I decide to act or not, I am making a decision with adequate knowledge of the situation. But the evils of humankind—how do I know about them? How do I know that I know enough to speak or act in any matter? In all public matters we are dependent on the presentation of news by the media; we have no firsthand knowledge. Newspapers and television not only present us with the facts but also with commentary to accompany the facts. There is no other way we can get acquainted with the problems of our world village. Personally, while being glad that modern newsgathering is so good, I am constantly filled with suspicion that I am not being given, cannot be given, the whole story. This makes me cautious of making moral judgments about situations outside my local community. I think this caution is necessary for us all in our appraisal of public situations. The subsidiary danger to this is that of bias. None of us is without bias. It affects our judgments of situations. Two persons in

the face of the same set of facts are likely to make quite different judgments because of their preconceived opinions.
(This happens in our house when we watch television
newscasts together.) Even more insidiously our biases can
determine whether or not we look at the facts in the first
place. We all need an incentive to be interested in issues, and
often it is our prejudices rather than our judgments which
provide this. This results in selective concern and indignation. Those who are concerned about the condition of the
people under South American right-wing dictatorships are
often unconcerned about injustice suffered by people in the
countries of the communist bloc, and vice versa. I suppose
this is a simple fact of human nature and little can be done
about it. Nevertheless I think that the little that can be done
has to be done; otherwise our moral judgments and actions
remain imperfect, and to that degree fall short of true Christian discipleship.

Jesus Christ must be our model. He was concerned
about public matters. I do not think we can say about him
that his "business was the relationship of the individual to
God. He wasn't there to change society." As we have seen,
the distinction between changing people and changing society did not exist in Jesus' time in Israel. The two went
together. It could never be said that Jesus was concerned only
about individuals and not about society. He took compassion
on the individuals he came across and healed them. But he
also taught them, and what he taught had a direct political
content: the purification of society and the ushering in of the
reign of God as a corporate concern. So much was he bound
up with the task of inaugurating this new kingdom that even
his individual acts of healing and compassion had a social impact because they were directed toward the outcasts of society and in associating with them and healing them Jesus was
making a set of conscious political statements. His opponents
recognized this and saw to it that he was done away with "for
the sake of the nation."

On the other hand it is anachronistic, and shallow, to

see Jesus as a political agent out to change society like any modern activist. He was a man of God. His ideas came from his prayer experience of union with the Father. The Father's will was Jesus' sole concern. For that he was prepared to do anything, even, in the end, to die. The kingdom Jesus preached was one where the Father's will was to be obeyed as religiously on earth as it is obeyed in heaven. Jesus spoke the language of spirituality; consequently his words penetrated deeper than any mere political speeches. They spoke to the parts of the human person which no politician ever reaches. They inspired men and women to surrender themselves religiously to God. They inspired people to pray. In listening to Jesus' words his disciples must not begin at the political end. If they do that they may not go deep enough to understand his true message. At some point their own political interests and prejudices will take over and thereafter their actions will be only Christian on the surface, Christian in label, not in content. The true disciple of Jesus must begin where he himself began: in prayer and fasting and reception of the Spirit. What follows will then be from God. We may be certain that disciples who begin with prayer will not be allowed to stop there, but will be led on through the challenges of personal morality to those of public morality. They will end up faced with political decisions as well as personal decisions. Both kinds of decision, however, will be spiritual ones. They will stem from a conversion of the heart toward God. That is what ushers in the reign of God which Jesus preached. Without a spiritual conversion it is not God's kingdom but merely a manmade replica which may look Christian on the surface but is at a deeper level merely secular.

Village concerns

To say that the true disciple of Jesus will be expected to make political decisions is a frightening remark. I find it frightening myself, being the sort of person who is not particularly interested in politics. Is there no place in the kingdom for those who mind their own business and leave

politics to the professionals and those who are interested?
Can some of us not opt out of the politics of Christian
discipleship and try harder in the areas of personal charity to
make up for it? Must Christians all be the same? Clearly we
are all made by God differently, and among the enormously
varied types of human beings only some are given the gifts
which equip them for careers in political activity. Only some,
therefore, are expected by God to be active politically for the
kingdom. (Only some are called to enter enclosed monaster-
ies for the kingdom.) Those of us, however, who are not ac-
tivists have a duty to be aware of the political dimensions of
Christian faith. We cannot, with a clear conscience, opt out
of that aspect of Christianity on the grounds that it does not
interest us. We cannot choose not to know.

A problem arises at this point for conscientious Christians. In the normal situation, coping with our lives, work
and neighborhood gives us more than enough to worry about
in terms of following Christ. No one has solved all his or her
problems, there is plenty yet to tackle, whether in the family,
or at work (or unemployed), or among neighbors. A preacher
could preach every Sunday for a year and still have more to
say about the gospel in the lives of his flock. It is tempting to
accept that and therefore remain with those subjects which
are immediately relevant to us all. The same goes for the
adult education program of a parish. Here also our local lives
provide enough to discuss and pray about without adding the
complications of wider issues about which we know very little. Nevertheless those wider issues cannot be ignored. They
have to be remembered (that can be painful), studied (that
means work), and prayed about (more work and pain).
However seductive the call to stay with the local material of
our lives, we have to resist it and think beyond our own
horizons. To do less than that would be to pass by on the
other side of the road while brothers and sisters living in the
same world with us lie broken in need of help.

In practice in our parish we have worked out a
minimum of subjects which we think every Christian should

be informed about in today's world. No follower of Jesus
Christ, no parishioner, we think, should turn a blind eye to
these matters. They must be constantly in our homilies and
discussions, in our prayers, and in our consciences as we look
for action to be done about them. They constitute a widening
of our horizons, but a widening toward our Christian responsibilities, not away from them. This is the list: The World
Village, Economic Colonialism, the Arms Trade, Racism,
Planet Earth. Readers may wish to add to this list, which is
perfectly acceptable. To subtract from the list is not,
however, acceptable. This list is the minimum for anyone today who takes the gospel seriously. The subjects are not optional extras to the good Christian life. They are part of the
life itself.

We live in the world village. According to the Brandt
Report (1980) the north end of the village has a quarter of the
population but enjoys 80% of the world income (and uses
85% of the oil). In the south end of the village live three-
quarters of the population, who have to make do with 20%
of the income. We live in the rich end of the village. According to economists the rich end of the village is growing richer,
but the poor end is not also getting richer, keeping in step
with us; it is getting poorer. Furthermore, this imbalance is a
seesaw. The poor (75%) are getting poorer because we (25%)
are getting richer. Our riches cause their poverty. As our
standard of living goes up in the seesaw, theirs goes down.
This horrifying fact is the reason why the need for us to do
something about the world imbalance is a question not of
charity but of simple justice. These world village facts are not
truths which we can be interested in or not as we choose.
Those who follow Christ and remember his parable about
Dives and Lazarus have to keep them in mind. They are on
the agenda of our judgment by God which he is making now.

One of the reasons why there is this imbalance between
North and South in our world is the continuing strength of
economic colonialism. Political colonialism has died.
Developed countries in the West no longer govern

undeveloped colonies in the Third World. For the most part there is self-government politically in Africa and Asia. But there is still what can be called economic colonialism. The new countries still depend on the West economically and are exploited, frankly, both as workers (for instance in tea) and consumers (for instance in baby food or cigarettes). Third World countries are governed economically from the United States and Europe probably as tightly as they were before they gained their political independence. A few years ago our parish became interested in tea. Observers from the World Development Movement had been to tea estates in Bangladesh owned by a British firm and had brought back information about the exploitation of workers on these British-owned tea estates. The workers were being paid grimly low wages and housed in appalling conditions—all in the interests of keeping the tea in our shops at an economical price. Workers in our country can no longer be treated in such a 19th-century manner, but foreign workers out of sight in a poor Third World country can. When challenged at the annual general meeting of the company, the chairman replied that his company was in the tradition of the Merchant Adventurers who had made Britain great in the past and had no intention of changing now. His first duty was to his shareholders not to Bangladesh tea workers. It was a brave, romantic response, but its real meaning was exploitation. The multinational companies of the West are engaged all the time in this exploitation of starvation-level workers at the poor end of our village in the interests of economic prosperity at the rich end. To know about this is a necessary part of being a follower of Jesus today. That Lazarus is out of sight must not mean that he is out of mind.

The arms trade is a postwar development in many Western nations. Not only does our armaments industry manufacture powerful, sophisticated weapons, aircraft, missiles and guns for the defense forces of our own country, but we also engage in trade to sell these weapons to foreign governments in the developing nations, like the Arab states.

This helps us to balance our national budget. There is often a triumphant headline in the news when a successful arms deal is brought off. The motive clearly is to make money. It is important for us that these poorer nations should buy weapons from our country, not from another, and to this end a vigorous sales campaign is maintained. Weapons to kill people are one of our more valuable exports. It is scarcely possible to square this national activity with the following of the gospel. It is another form of cynical exploitation of the poor in order to preserve the affluence of the rich.

Racism is the fourth on the list of world evils which we encourage our parish to know about. There is racism which is built into the laws of a nation as in South Africa today. There is also the racism which can inhabit the individual heart, whatever the laws of the country. This can result in a whole set of customs, taboos, unwritten laws and accepted practices which can effectively exclude people from justice on the grounds of their race. Both aspects of racism need to be spotlighted and combated by followers of Jesus. Jesus stood for the breaking of all taboos which prevent people from being respected and which prevent true community from being formed.

The last on our list of public moral issues which cannot be ignored is the issue of planet Earth: How we should treat the created world which God has given us as a sacred responsibility. The exploitation we have to combat here is not a direct exploitation of people, as in economic colonialism or the arms trade, but the exploitation of Mother Earth. Ecologists are sometimes regarded as freaks, but their concern is not an eccentric hobby. It is an issue of central importance. The 20th century has seen an exploitation of nature by the rich countries which is unparalleled and gigantic. Coal, oil, gasoline, natural gas, fresh water (by pollution), trees and soil have been plundered by the industrial nations to provide the affluence they require. And it seems to be increasing beyond control. One does not have to believe in God to be saddened and sickened by what we are doing to our planet.

If, in addition, the person knows that God creates the planet and creates human beings to exercise responsibility for it, the sickening and saddening is accompanied by fear. What will God say to our reckless selfishness?

The above is only a quick sketch of the issues which I think no disciple of Christ can ignore without guilt. Many would add abortion and the nuclear bomb to the list. It is essential to know about these problems. To avoid thinking about them, either because they seem too remote from our day-to-day lives or because we can do nothing about them, is a step toward running away from Christianity. To be aware, then, of these world issues is the first step in Christian responsibility. The second step is to be clear, not vague, about our involvement in these evils. Here two dangers are to be avoided. One danger is the emotional one of being so struck by the evil, and our involvement in it, that we begin to use the word *sinful* recklessly. It is not helpful or accurate to make everyone feel guilty all the time. We have to be careful here. The whole situation is, indeed, sinful and involves guilt. There are those whose connection with it does mean sin: the direct exploiters in industry and government. The majority of people, however, are not directly sinning. It is not a sin every time we drink a cup of tea, even though that tea has come from the tea estates in the Third World to our supermarkets by a chain involving injustice. I do not think it helpful or particularly Christian to bandy the word *sin* about and make people feel guilty in this matter. On the other hand, a second danger is to adopt the opposite attitude of saying the whole thing has nothing to do with us because it is beyond our control. We cannot wash our hands of responsibility so easily. The world of industry and commerce and politics is intricately interrelated, and we in the rich countries benefit from that system. Our standard of living is maintained by it. If we benefit materially from the connections of commerce, we must also accept the connections of moral responsibility. We *are* involved, if not in personal sin, then in a sinful situation. In other words, in these matters of universal injustice we have to face up to the facts of universal inter-relatedness of responsibility and, as Christians, refer ourselves to Christ's call to love all people and inaugurate his kingdom of peace, love and justice. Today, perhaps, we need a new category of responsibility to help us understand our Christian duty in our interconnected world. Somewhere between personal sin and personal sinlessness there are attitudes and actions which involve us indirectly in gross sin. Our consciences therefore require us to do something, act or register protest, even while we continue to go about our daily lives. It is not sinful every time we drink tea, but perhaps it is sinful to do so continually without protest. The mobilizing of public opinion by protest is an important Christian action at times, simply because it is often the only available action. You and I, for instance, can do nothing directly about the racism of the South African state. But we can protest. In a democracy politicians listen to protest when it comes from a sufficient number of voters.

In these matters Christians are not alone in their protest. They find themselves alongside many people of good will who are not Christians. In many cases the Christians are running to catch up with their non-Christian companions who are ahead of them in zeal and awareness. My experience is that Christians can make two important contributions to these struggles. The first contribution is hope. A big temptation to the worker in the field of international justice is to despair. The problems seem so enormous and intractable. The human capacity for wickedness seems so limitless: war, plunder, selfishness, cruelty, dishonesty with themselves, larger and larger with each succeeding year. Those who fight against it seem so small, ineffectual, helpless. "Where do we begin?" is a familiar cry in our parish groups when they discuss these matters. The individual citizen appears so small and government so big when it comes to talking about the arms trade, multinational exploitation, or the racial state of South Africa. The only answer to this is Christian hope. God is on our side, however faithless we prove to be. Trust in the future; trust in the fundamental goodness and reasonableness of humanity—both are guaranteed by Christ and his Father. The distinctive contribution of Christians to the struggle for peace and justice has to be hope. A glance at the crucifix on the wall should always be sufficient to remind us that God is not defeated, in the long term, by the force of human selfishness, however hopeless the short-term prospect. Since the resurrection we have no need to run away from Gethsemane when the cause seems lost.

The second distinctive Christian contribution to the cause of peace and justice is love. It is easy, unfortunately, for an enterprise in the cause of justice which begins in love to end in envy and hatred of opponents. The pressures of working against heavy odds with little encouragement can have a deteriorating effect on those who campaign. Against opposition and selfishness from powerful interests we can too easily respond with malice. When this happens something goes out of the struggle, a purity and nobility which, though often impractical, prevents us from using evil weapons to fight evil, trying to beat the Devil at his own game. Only love, simple Christian love, can combat this. It is the most difficult virtue to maintain under pressure; but it is the one most needed. Working in this cause we have reason to recall that "love bears all things, believes all things, hopes all things, endures all things." When we are confronted with those "all things" in the shape of powerful moneyed interests and organized selfishness, it is an opportunity for us to witness to our belief that Christ has "overcome the world" and that love is more powerful than hate. This challenge is, of course, the very point where we touch Christ and live the paschal mystery to the full.

EIGHT:

Change

A well-known graffito goes, Just when I thought I had all the answers to my life, they changed the questions. Whoever the anonymous sufferer was, he or she was responding accurately to the pressures of life today. We live in an age of change when even the most stable traditions in our society are being questioned. Perhaps all ages are ages of change, but there is no doubt that some periods are marked by change more than others. Our age is one of those. We live in a period of cultural transition. Most of the fundamental values by which our fathers and mothers lived, which they accepted without demur, are now being questioned, being changed, being exposed—values having to do with family life, education, social intercourse, patriotism, religion. If *sacred* means "revered" and "accepted as absolute," then our age is the age when nothing is sacred any longer. All is subject to criticism and possible rejection. Culture is beginning to shift, leaving the past behind and developing toward an unknown future.

Depending on our years, and even more on our temperaments, we react to this fact of universal change with excitement or horror. The important thing, however, in the face of change, is to dip below the surface reactions. Human beings are asked to respond at a more serious level than mere temperament to the challenge of change. That being so, it is useful to devote a chapter to the phenomenon of change in our society, both secular and ecclesiastical. It is one of the key ways in which we live out the paschal mystery and grow closer to the crucified, now risen, Christ (a man of change if ever there was one).

Change in any society takes place when a sufficient number of members asks the question, *Why do we do that?*

When in the '60s a sufficient number of nuns asked, *Why do we wear these 17th-century habits and headdresses?* a change was in the cards. Before long a revolutionary transformation of religious dress took place. The radical question, of course, is not always followed by change. Sometimes a suggestion is answered negatively and the traditional way of doing things retained; change is rejected, and in the rejection society has been deepened and renewed in its course of action. This happened in the '60s over prayer. A large number of Christians asked, *Why pray at all? Why not make our whole life prayer and give up the specific act of praying in the gaps of life?* Popular books were written which denied the value of prayer as it had traditionally been practiced. Much debate went on, but in the end the traditional ideas prevailed and the new ones were rejected. In the '70s prayer flooded back as a more important activity than ever all over the Christian world. Radical questioning, therefore, is not necessarily a sign that change will automatically take place. It is, properly speaking, a sign of seriousness rather than change.

Two kinds of questions can be asked of a society. There are "how" questions and "whether" questions. How questions are not radical, but practical. They presume the system and ask how to make it work. They spring from anxiety as all questioning does, but it is anxiety centering on personal worthiness. It does not question the value of the system, but the person's own value within the system. How questions are questions of individual adjustment. A new recruit to a business constantly asks this type of question: *How am I doing? How am I fitting in? Am I learning all right?* Of course how questions can also be communal. *How is the firm doing? How can we stabilize the economy? How can we recruit more novices into the congregation?* They are practical questions which assume a given system.

Whether questions do not presume the system and therefore are not immediately practical. They go to the root of the system (are radical) and ask whether the system is worth having or not. They, too, spring from anxiety, anxiety about whether the system is worthwhile at all. The criticism engendered by whether questions is a criticism of the system itself, not of individual members within it. Not *How do I fit into this business?* but *Is the business worth having? Is it doing a relevant job?* Clearly these are more radical, and therefore more threatening than simple how questions. When novices in a religious congregation begin to question age-old novitiate practices, rather than questioning their own performance of them, novice masters feel threatened. Radical questions often come as a surprise. The parish priest who asks his assistant to look after the Mothers' Club is surprised if the assistant questions whether it is a good thing to have a Mothers' Club in the first place. In *Searching for God*, his published addresses as abbot to Ampleforth monks, Cardinal Hume notes how the novices of the '60s reversed the customary process and instead of offering themselves for judgment by the community seemed to be themselves judging the community.

Little change at the level of community takes place from how questioning, which of its nature is geared to personal improvement. It is whether questions which inaugurate community changes. They are the radical questions which go to the root of established custom. They are the valuable questions at a time of cultural transition. A few comments may therefore be in order:

1. Once asked, whether questions cannot be ignored. It is no use saying, "Keep quiet." They have to be considered and taken seriously. They will not go away by being ignored. For instance, the question, *Should women be ordained priests?* does not disappear if no one answers it. It has been asked and therefore must be debated. The last thirty years have seen many such questions in the Catholic church centering around Latin in the liturgy, rule by encyclical, priestly celibacy and intercommunion with other Christians, to mention but a few. The church has been a wise mother when she has allowed open debates on these matters.

2.   There is a need not only to put up with radical questions but to promote them. They are good things, signs of
strength in the church, not regrettable necessities or signs of
weak faith. Without the radical questioning of the pioneer
thinkers of the 1940s and 1950s, the Catholic church would
not have made the advances she made at the Vatican Council. We today are the grateful heirs of those earlier questioners.

3.   The authority which listens openly to radical questions is credible today. The authority which does not is simply not credible. To slap down dissent at the first sign does
not inspire confidence. It is seen as a sign of weakness, not
strength, in a ruler. People nowadays are quick to smell out
fear in their leaders. Let us be frank and admit that there is
much of this fear in the church today. It is difficult to cope
with fear in a position of leadership. It is not easy to be objective about criticism, and all too easy to run away from the
problems. It is interesting to notice that the radical ideas
which we ourselves produce hold no fear for us, so we live
happily with them and are eager to promote them. But
radical ideas from others we greet with suspicion. They are
new to us; it takes time for us to overcome our fears and
discuss them openly.

4.   Some people today wonder whether, in view of the
importance of radical questioning in the church to further
the kingdom and prevent stagnation and corruption, a case
can be made for writing it into the structures of the institution. The mature democracies of the West have evolved in
the course of history, not without wars and wounds, the concept of the loyal Opposition. In Great Britain, for example,
the Leader of the Opposition is a paid, respected, public servant. In the United States the House or Senate Minority
Leader holds a position of power. We regard a nation where
opposition is treated with death or imprisonment as immature. We think that leaders who react by putting their opponents in prison or stripping them of their functions are

primitive and have much to learn. By being afraid of criticism they deprive themselves of the precious advantage of open discussion and frank exchange of views. Can a case be made for the same development in the church? This is a matter worth airing in debate and is not as bizarre as it may at first appear, although perhaps by its very nature radical thinking is charismatic and would be tamed by institutionalization. The idea of an official opposition in a diocese is probably too structured for the purposes of the kingdom. Nevertheless genuine opposition has surely to be welcomed, because it is only by radical questioning that the church progresses and keeps faith with her Lord. Only thus can she be *semper reformanda et reformata.* In a diocese or parish both opposition and establishment are inspired by the Holy Spirit. Personally I find that an awesome and inspiring thought.

There is need for a spirituality of radical questioning, both for those who are questioned and those who do the questioning. Criticism is a work of the Spirit and should be taken seriously. For those who engage in radical questioning there is a prime necessity that they do it in love. Criticism in love is valuable and fruitful. Criticism without love is not, because it comes from an unpurified heart and can be a front for less than Christian, mediocre sentiments. If the heart is not purified from rebellious pride, vainglory, malice and similar imperfections, our criticisms will not be helpful; they will simply be a way of letting off steam on our part, a form of ego trip which makes us feel good but is harmful to the common cause. Much harm can be done by such posturing. It would be sad if we engaged in that sort of behavior and thought ourselves to be radical critics with an important message. We have to purify the sources of our criticism, for unspiritual questioning is as corrupting as the unspiritual exercise of power. When in a mood to be critical it is helpful to ask ourselves questions like this: *Do I really want to help or am I just letting off steam? Would I be prepared to give time and work to implement my suggestions, or are they mere words? Would I work in the background and be prepared for others to receive the publicity and praise, or am I aiming at glory for myself? Am I flexible in my suggestions, or am I hard and immovable?* These and similar questions can serve to help us be honest with ourselves in our radical aims and to kindle love in our hearts toward those we criticize. In the church the critic has always to ask: How do I criticize my mother?

For the radical questioner it is important that his whether questions be accompanied by how questions. Faced with an imperfect situation which calls for radical criticism the temptation is to shelve all matters of personal effort until the basic issue has been tackled. This is temptingly logical but not very Christian or mature. Most generations of university students produce radical criticisms of the teaching and examining systems of their university: too many essays to write, the exam system is an inefficient and unfair way of finding out what they know, and so forth. The immediate temptation is to stop all work until the system is overhauled. It does not take much insight to see that such logical action leads nowhere and could be very mixed in motive. The mature course is to continue to work under the imperfect system while aiming for a better one. If we all quit working until the perfect system had been achieved, nothing would ever get done, because the search for the perfect system is never finished. In other words whether questioning has to be accompanied by the continuation of honest how questioning in order to ensure personal probity. The two kinds of criticism, criticism of the institution and criticism of self, work best when they accompany each other and feed each other mutually. Church renewal and personal renewal go hand in hand and need each other. This is especially true in the enterprise of following Christ. None of us is perfect, so as we criticize the institution we must not relax in self-criticism; otherwise we run into pride and vanity which are obstacles to the Spirit in our work. If, for instance, as a priest I wish to question the way authority is exercised in the Catholic church, it is more effective if I do this from a position of having kept my promise of obedience to my bishop than if I am a self-indulgent character who cannot be trusted to obey. In the latter case my criticism is bound up with the search to make life easier for myself rather than with the cause of making Christ's kingdom come. My arguments are not very convincing if I have unilaterally anticipated their outcome in my personal life. The inspiring thing about the radical pioneers of the Vatican Council was that they proved they could live obediently in the unreformed church while they worked for reform. Their personal probity gave a special effectiveness to their call for reform. Obedience is universally more creative than disobedience in the kingdom of God.

We participate in Christ's paschal mystery when with sincerity we engage in criticism in the church or in society. We also touch Christ when we are at the receiving end of radical questioning, whether it comes from others or from our own conscience. Jesus underwent the heart searching which accompanies all new ideas. We must not think that his program of reform for Judaism came to him wrapped in a package, down from the heavens, with no struggle. His ideas must have been thought out and prayed over for years before he began to promulgate them. Some of those meditations were surely painful, for Jesus was fully human. The fears of Gethsemane and Calvary were the last, but certainly not the first, of his heart searchings. Brought up a law-abiding Jew, he cannot have found it easy to break away from his background, even though he enjoyed a unitive experience in prayer with the Father. It was that experience of union which gave him the conviction that his campaign for the new reign of God came from God. But he still had to undergo the suspicion of his relatives who thought he was mad, and the incomprehension of his own people in Nazareth, then he had to face the hostility of the priests in Jerusalem. To inaugurate the kingdom and redeem us Jesus had to suffer, not just physically but in the pit of his stomach too.

Radical questioning directed toward ourselves can be the bitterest of suffering. It pulls the carpet from under us and makes our hearts sink. These metaphors only partly portray the despair that can grip us when precious securities are taken away. In the church many in this generation have undergone that form of cross as ancient traditions have been destroyed and new, unattractive usages appeared in their place. The anguish that some have felt over the disappearance of the Latin liturgy is only one of many such experiences. Most priests could make a list of losses which have been sustained by older Catholics in the post-Vatican II generation. We could also testify to a wonderful, faithful acceptance of new, not fully understood ways in a manner which puts many ecclesiastics to shame. We encounter inspiring trust in God among the people. In our personal lives, too, we are asked to undergo many deaths in the course of Christian discipleship. Not only precious customs of the past but also present securities are assailed in day-to-day living. All of us are asked from time to time to face hostility and remain loving even while our inner self is seething with violent feelings or melting away in despair. Acceptance of the cross in union with Jesus Christ is not, however, meant to be a question of gritting our teeth in a hard struggle. We are asked, in union with Christ, to be patiently loving and to embrace the cross creatively. All crosses, or deaths, change us. We have to practice being changed neither in a passive manner nor with a bitter fight, but gently and openly, letting go to God in complete trust. We have to be "crucified with Christ" in union with his own faithful surrender to the Father on Calvary.

One area in modern society where how questions are being superseded by whether questions is marriage. In the past marriage was a stable institution throughout Christendom. Couples in the course of their married life asked themselves plenty of how questions: *How are we getting along? Are we good for each other? Are we good parents to our children? How can we improve?* But whether they should remain married was not often a question which arose. Society did not permit that. Today it is different. Society countenances divorce. So, from the beginning, from the first quarrel, the whether question now lurks in the background of marriage. Not *How can we make it up?* but *Should we perhaps get a divorce?* is the question now near the surface when quarrels happen. This makes marriages insecure in their roots from the start. Spouses are liable to undergo that experience of pit-of-the-stomach despair with a frequency that their grand-parents never knew. In a growing number of cases, even among Christians, this results in the end of the marriage. It is noteworthy, however, that today's radical questioning in marriages calls forth a depth of commitment and a growth in grace which was less known in former, more stable, times. The temptation to abandon the marriage is also the oppor-tunity to renew it at the roots. When brought to the brink of giving the partnership up, then couples are able to remake the original decision to enter into it, and so at the root the marriage begins again to grow. On the one hand, in terms of quantity, marriages are less stable than in the past. On the other hand, in terms of quality, the sacrament of marriage is perhaps healthier. Married couples live out their sacrament deeply and with a conscious cooperation with grace which is remarkable. The paschal mystery thus reaches unparalleled fulfilment in Christian marriages today. The deaths involved in radical questioning have resulted in inspiring resurrec-tions. The Marriage Encounter movement is an optimistic symbol of what is occurring in many families. It is one of the witnesses to the change for the better which radical question-ing produces.

Another instance of radical questioning leading to deeper commitment has been in the celibate priesthood of the Catholic church. There has been radical questioning about celibacy in recent years. Defections from the priesthood have received much publicity. This is natural and healthy. To have tried to hide them would have been the unhealthy thing. Publicity has not, understandably, been given to numbers of celibate priests who have remained faithful to their priestly promises in spite of pulls in the other direc-tion—it would be far from true to think that only those

priests who left underwent struggles of conscience. Our ad-
miration goes to those priests who have experienced strong
emotional attraction to abandon their celibacy, who have
suffered sometimes to the breaking point in the church which
they experience as corrupt, but who have stayed faithful to
their commitment for positive reasons. They are unsung
heroes. Their reward has been not public acclaim but inner
deepening of their priestly vocations. They would not wish
any other reward. Like those spouses who have been faithful
through marital rough weather, they have experienced for
themselves the fruits of the paschal mystery, the richly
renewed life in Christ which only comes after generously accepted death in Christ. The important changes we undergo
as Christians are not the external changes which take place in
church life, or even in liturgy and devotions, but the inner
changes of heart and soul of which the structural changes are
surface symbols. Living the paschal mystery of Christ is a call
to undergo those inner changes. Only they penetrate to the
roots of our being and can in the last analysis be called
radical. The final truth about change is that it takes place only in order that we may become more deeply what we are.
Change in the church, and in her individual members, is the
way God the Father invites us to become more radically what
we already are: his children. It is a disaster, then, to be too
timid to face up to change. Courage to face change and accept it from God is the supreme blessing.

NINE:

Love,
Death and
Resurrection

EMBRACING THE CROSS

Preachers, following St. Paul, are fond of the theme of dying in order that we may live. The old man has to die in order that the new man may live. According to St. Paul, this death to the old ways of nature needs to be consciously linked with the historical death of Jesus on the cross so that the new life we hope to be given after our deaths may be linked with the present life of the risen Jesus Christ, the life of grace. Spiritual death leading to spiritual life—that is the theme of paschal mystery. The parable from St. John's gospel of the grain of wheat dying in order that it may burgeon and bear fruit is a classic exposition of this idea. How often we hear it in the pulpit and use it in counselling others.

It is important to handle this theme of spiritual death with care; otherwise we may take wrong turnings in our eagerness to follow Jesus Christ. One wrong turn is that of fatalism. Fatalism, as its name implies, means being passive under the hand of Fate, doing nothing to fight disaster or evil, just accepting what happens as the unchangeable will of God. For some people, this is seductively attractive. They come up against a natural or a manmade disaster and yield to it in holy abandon. *This is the cross*, they say to themselves. *We must embrace it. This is what God wants. It would be wrong to fight it. A follower of Jesus must surrender.* Just because this reaction looks so Christian and uses so effectively the language of mysticism, it is important to combat it and show how unchristian it is, and how unmystical.

Christianity is not a religion of fatalism. Jesus never passively accepted evil but fought against it and expected his followers to do likewise. When he found sick people he did not urge them to accept their condition; he encouraged them to have faith that they could be better and cured them. When he saw injustice he spoke out against it. His active struggle against evil and corruption was, as we saw, the very thing that brought him to the cross. If he had been a fatalist and accepted the state of Jewish religion in his day without murmur and in "holy surrender," he would have died peacefully in his bed; there would have been no cross, and we would not have heard of him. By the phrase, "taking up the cross," he did not mean any notion of passive acceptance of evil. What he meant was active acceptance of the hardships involved in promoting the kingdom. Jesus, in other words, saw the cross, his cross and our cross, not as an end in itself, not as a good thing to be aimed at, but as a necessary evil to be endured for the sake of the greater good he was pursuing. Being fully human and normal, he would have liked to avoid his passion, the dreadful public humiliation, the torture of the scourging, crowning with thorns, crucifixion, but they became necessary stations on the road he had to pass through so he embraced them. He was not embracing death as an end in itself, but as the last means left to spread his message, and the ultimate consecration of his mission.

As Christians we must follow Jesus in this and learn to discern when to fight and when to surrender, what we should accept and what we should resist. We should be completely non-accepting of evils and all lack of love in and around ourselves. Here there must be a fight, which means the rejection of all forms of fatalism. The language of fatalism sounds in phrases like *You can't change the world, You must be realistic, practical, There's no hope of an alteration in that quarter, There's nothing new under the sun, We must live with what we've got.* With phrases like those we quiet our consciences or silence others who disturb us. We have to recognize this fatalistic voice when we hear it and, following the example of Christ, reject it. Imagine him saying we can't change the world! So we must never yield to the attraction to do nothing about wrongs and call that embracing the cross. Some years ago I gave a retreat to an enclosed community of contemplatives. In that community was a social abuse which had imperceptibly grown, as can so easily happen. All the members of the community knew about the abuse, but nothing was being done because to correct it would have been very difficult, very far from "practical." I found that the members were opting to do nothing on the grounds that they had entered the community to embrace the cross of Christ and must not pull back in the face of it. They were "offering up" the situation in holy abandon. It seemed to me that in reality what was happening was that everyone was, understandably, too frightened to take the necessary Christian action and was hiding behind the concept of the cross of Christ, using it in a way which Christ would not have done. The community members were taking the easier of two paths, the line of least resistance, and calling it acceptance of the cross. This was a misunderstanding about the meaning of taking up the cross to follow Christ. It was equated with doing nothing in the face of evil. But Jesus did not accept evils in the name of the cross. He fought them. He did not tell people to live in society with injustice; he said they were blessed if they hungered and thirsted after justice.

Christians have to resist evil in all its forms. What we have to be accepting of is the setbacks and hardships which come with the fight. Here the idea of cross and death is appropriate. We will have many crosses, encounter many diminishments to our pride, self-esteem, even our health, if we follow Jesus. No suffering ought to be too great for us to bear patiently and without complaint in our pursuit of the kingdom. The trouble is that we tend to find ourselves resisting when we should be accepting, and accepting when we should be resisting. Our fears and laziness encourage us to do nothing about the evils we meet in society and in ourselves precisely when we should do something; contrariwise our selfishness encourages us to wriggle out of hardships when the Christian solution is to embrace them for the sake of the struggle. In both cases fear has made us unlike Christ, lazily accepting when we should be combative, and combative when we should be generously accepting. We accept the wrong sort of death (evil) but run away from the right sort of death (diminishment of self in the cause of the kingdom).

The key to understanding the Christian attitude to suffering, the cross, is to remember that Jesus never embraced it as an end in itself, but he always embraced it as a means to a good end, the spread of the kingdom. If we understand that, we shall avoid two errors of the last hundred years. Nineteenth-century Christianity tended to make death and suffering the end in itself of the good life. Too much was written and preached about the desirability of suffering as if it were a good thing in itself. The religious art of the period strikingly manifests this preoccupation with passion and blood. The 20th century also falls into the error of making suffering an end in itself, but it reacts in the opposite way: It wants to abolish it, and makes that a chief aim in life. Our generation is enormously concerned with the removal of all suffering, even when it is a necessary stage on the road to perfection and fulfilment. Our generation wants to avoid suffering altogether, and in doing so avoids growth too. We have reacted against the 19th-century glorification of suffering by simply eliminating it altogether. For instance, much medical and social work today is geared to pain-killing rather than painful healing. Abortion and euthanasia are examples of this. We prefer to avoid pain rather than find a cure for a painful situation. Easy divorce is another example. We eliminate the problem instead of looking for a solution. Neither the 19th- nor the 20th-century attitude to pain is Christian. Both err because they make too much of the means, suffering, and not enough of the end, which is perfection and fulfilment. The genuine Christian attitude is the optimistic one of aiming at human growth with the clear-sighted recognition that that will mean the acceptance of much suffering on the way. The cross is the necessary means to Christian maturity, but certainly not its end. The grain of wheat dies only in order to increase and multiply.

Properly understood pain, the cross, is a watering of the roots of growth. We cannot do without the cross. It both fertilizes us and purifies us. This is a constant theme in the Bible from the Exodus story onwards. Their stay in the desert "made" the People of God. Their later exile to Babylon further purified and spiritualized them. In both cases it is interesting to note, the Jews moaned and groaned at the time about what was happening to them and only later recognized how valuable it was. That is how we often react to the cross: at first resistance, then acceptance, then praise for its therapeutic effect. The child at first resists becoming an adult but soon learns not to look back but go ahead joyfully. Some may remember learning to ride a bicycle, how terrified we were at first when the supporting hand of a parent was withdrawn, how we shouted for it to stay at our back. But then, when we found we could do without that support, how we resented any attempt to make us go back to our earlier state of protection and thought we had always wanted freedom.

So much of Christian acceptance of pain is a question of learning to live with our fears. I do not like the phrase *conquer fear*; it implies a combative gritting of the teeth which in my experience serves to make one more tense and more fearful. The best way to handle the fears that all of us have is to let go. It has to be a movement of relaxation or, better still, a movement of trust. This does not eliminate our fears; nothing does. But it helps us to live with and through them calmly. In the midst of fear we make ourselves trust the Father, reminding ourselves, and him, that he holds us in the hollow of his hand, completely circling us with his love. This is what Jesus did, not without a struggle, in Gethsemane and in that last cry on the cross: "Father, into thy hands I commit my spirit." Taking up the cross as disciples of Jesus means imitating him in that, which is the heart of discipleship. In that way we learn not to eliminate pain and fear in our lives, but to pass calmly through them and to grow in the experience in a manner we never could if we repressed the cross and turned our backs every time we met it.

Letting go is the way we grow as Christians. The old saying, A bird in the hand is worth two in the bush, reflects our native reluctance to grow. It reflects a mean, cautious, all-too-human spirit of clinging to what we have in case we should lose it. It is a refusal to take a risk and so to grow. Suppose you want to increase and grow? Suppose you want those two birds in the bush? You cannot move without first making the decision to release the bird you hold in your hand. For a moment you will be without anything, your hands empty. Furthermore there is the possibility you may not catch those two birds in the bush; you may end up worse off than ever, with nothing. Faced with that possibility many decide to stay with what they have, the one safely held bird. But the adventurous person decides to take a risk and go for the two birds. The cautious type is perhaps what we all are basically. There are not many naturally adventurous persons. Undoubtedly in the history of the church that safety-first clinging to possessions has been all too frequently predominant. There is, however, little doubt that the latter spirit is the spirit of Jesus and his gospel. He teaches us to take the risk, to let go and leave completely to the Father what happens next. He teaches us to trust. By letting go in Christ we grow spiritually. To grow and be free we have to cast our caution to one side and to let go into God. When Jesus did that on the cross it led to his resurrection. It will do the same for us in the many deaths that we face in our progress through life.

Our deaths

The doctrine of life through death is easier to preach than to practice. It is an ever-present challenge, because

there are few situations when God is not presenting us with
the cross-resurrection pattern and inviting us to make the
transition from one to the other by letting go. Bereavement is
an example. When we lose a beloved relative or friend, we
react with a numbed shock and are at first tempted to deny
what has happened. This is followed by fear and panic as we
look into a future which will not contain our beloved but be
desperately empty. The next step must then be to let go,
release, give that person back to God in a generous surrender.
If we back away from this out of resentment at the unilateral
action of God in taking our companion, we are condemning
ourselves to a life of unhappiness, to a life of bitter clinging to
the past which cannot come back. The only feasible course is
to release our spiritual hold on the dead person and give him
or her back to God. This is not easy and is not always immediately successful. We have to be gentle with ourselves
and persevere. We can be sure that God too is gentle with us
and will continue to help us to succeed and make allowances
for our stumbling. From the moment we try, we begin to
grow again and remake our broken life with serenity. This
new life may not look so full as the previous one, but it may
well be deeper and closer to God.

At other times in life we are asked to undergo a similar
experience when someone we love rejects us. As in bereavement the first reaction to this is often shock and denial. It
can't be true! Telephone calls are made, meetings arranged
in the attempt to disprove the rejection. Then, when the
truth can no longer be denied, we feel panic at the prospect
of the empty, single future ahead. The decisive moment is
when we choose to accept the situation, see that it is fundamentally ridiculous to cling to someone who does not want
us, and try to let go. As with bereavement we have to
persevere gently but firmly in this matter, and never lose our
confidence that God is with us, supporting and guiding.
Once again we are being given a lesson in the death-
resurrection experience. The lesson is a valuable lesson in

love, and may prove fruitful for marriage at a later date to someone else—the lesson that love is giving and letting go, not clinging possessively.

A third case of growth through death and resurrection is the experience which parents undergo when their children grow up. Books, plays and songs have been written on this familiar theme. It is worth noting that it is a situation in which not only the child but also the parent is being challenged to grow. Parents can remain childish and never grow into full adulthood when they refuse to let their children grow away from them. The casualties in possessive parenthood are not only the children but also the parents. C. Day Lewis wrote an attractive poem on the subject:

Walking Away

It is eighteen years ago, almost to the day—
A sunny day with the leaves just turning,
The touch-lines new-ruled—since I watched you play
Your first game of football, then, like a satellite
Wrenched from its orbit, go drifting away.

Behind a scatter of boys. I can see
You walking away from me towards the school
With the pathos of a half-fledged thing set free
Into a wilderness, the gait of one
Who finds no path where the path should be.

That hesitant figure, eddying away
Like a winged seed loosened from its parent stem,
Has something I never quite grasp to convey
About Nature's give-and-take—the small, the scorching
Ordeals which fire one's irresolute clay.

I have had worse partings, but none that so
Gnaws at my mind still. Perhaps it is roughly
Saying what God alone could perfectly show—
How selfhood begins with a walking away,
And love is proved in the letting go.

A special case of this growth through releasing another from dependence is the case of the confidant or counsellor. People come to us for help. We willingly give it and often it grows into a series of meetings as we support someone through a crisis. Then our friend begins no longer to need us, and, like a challenged parent, we have to let him or her go. If we do not, we harm both ourselves and the other person. It is not easy to let a dependant go, because in a subtle way we become dependent on our dependants. (This is especially the case with celibates, for obvious reasons.) The spiritual guide has to learn that success comes when he or she is no longer needed. It is a death we do not like to face, but there is no resurrection into maturity without it.

The experiences of bereavement, rejection or parenthood act as dress rehearsals for our own death. If we have taught ourselves to let go with trust in God as we undergo the "deaths" which those experiences bring us, we ought to be well prepared for the supreme experience of giving up our life into the hands of God. Except for those who die suddenly, death is not a quick event. It begins to happen in the second half of our life and approaches slowly, for some painfully slowly, and all too obviously. This experience of diminishment in the second half of our life is a fruitful area for spiritual growth. It is the time when the paschal mystery touches our lives most closely. It may be helpful to enumerate some ways in which death approaches, and to see how we can be faithful to God as it does so.

Our bodies begin to fail. Ailments multiply, not only big dramatic ones which land us in the hospital, but little, semi-hidden ones which are new irritants to our daily living. We cannot do what we used to be able to do. We need more rest and comfort. We need to be helped more often. All these are opportunities to swallow pride and accept gracefully the diminishments of our bodies. It is an occasion for going deeper in our assessments and learning that the love of God is measured by the heart and not by physical and ascetical achievement. It is not always easy to accept that our loving

Father is present in these "death" experiences. We tend to think in a primitive way that as our hold on physical life gets weaker, so our hold on spiritual life will too. But the opposite is more likely to be true. As we diminish physically we can be growing by giant strides spiritually. This only takes place, however, if we allow it to happen by letting go generously to God. The generous acceptance of bodily weakening leads to spiritual resurrection in our souls.

As we grow older our attraction for other people dies. It has been said, To look young is to be needed. When we no longer look young we experience more often being ignored in company, being taken for granted, not being needed. Our sexuality lessens, and with it that physical glow which is the natural, unself-conscious endowment of youth. With age the physical glow disappears, and, annoyingly, self-consciousness can increase just when we do not want it. Here, too, the Christian learns to accept the situation loving-ly from God and see it as a gift, an invitation to grow closer to the Father. The great gift of old age is that we are drawing closer to the Beatific Vision. It is worth accepting the diminishment of attractiveness to other people in return for that unbelievable gift of being attracted by God, and, in-deed, being attractive to him.

Another experience, as we age, is that all possible futures die. We wake up to the realization that there are now places in the world to which we shall never go, experiences we shall never have, careers which we have no chance of pur-suing. In this way the second half of life brings with it an in-creased dose of reality. We can no longer entertain ourselves with fantasies about other careers we could pursue or other places to go. We have to accept that we are stuck with the jobs, places, families we have—for life. This is experienced as a loss, but in fact is a gain. To live in the real world, free of fantasies, is itself an important step toward God. Thomas Merton said, "The monk begins to live the moment he wakes up and realizes he will never be a saint and never be abbot." This narrowing down of possibilities is at the same time an invitation to go deeper in our pursuit of life. All we have to do is to accept the fact graciously and let God's Spirit flood into our now more real lives.

The diminishment that most of us find hardest to accept as we grow older is not our bodily defects, but our gradual retirement from responsibility. The archetypal case is that of mothers whose responsibility for their children lessens with each year the child grows. For them retirement begins early! It happens, however, to everyone in every sphere of life sooner or later. We groan over our responsibilities and dream of carefree retirement while we are at work, but when we do retire we suffer greatly over the loss we looked forward to. The wise person keeps retirement in mind all the time, neither fantasizing over it as utopia, nor dreading it as death. Retirement *is* death, but Christian death, which is a life-giving encounter with Christ. Let us not treat retirement lightly; it involves much pain. To find oneself no longer in the center of events, to see crowds gathering around other leaders, listening to other voices, getting excited about new causes in which one plays no part—this is not easy. There is sometimes the temptation to try to recapture the excitement of earlier days by cynically denigrating the new movements, or by absurdly trying to stage a comeback into popularity. These reactions are immature. The mature reaction is, once again, acceptance, but positive, happy acceptance, not the bitter acceptance of resignation to the inevitable. Retirement from achievement and the limelight that goes with it is the call to place our value not in personal achievement but in God. We no longer are able to find ourselves in work, so we are drawn to find ourselves in the state of being children of our heavenly Father. Work, activity and achievement no longer give meaning to living because they no longer exist. There is a vacuum where they were in our lives. But we must have a meaning for living! So we are invited to find it in God, in simply being loved by him; not in doing things for him, but in receiving love from him. After a life of active living this is not easy. We so much prefer achieving things for God to

receiving gifts from him. Giving is good for our egos, receiving bad for them. This crisis is spiritually important, because
it is the moment in life when we realize the truth about grace
and salvation: They are gifts from God, not achievements on
our part. If we ever get to heaven it will be by God's love for
us, not our love for him. The diminishments of the second
half of our life are there to lead us into that truth. The gospel
parable of the workers in the vineyard is a test case for this
understanding. Many people find the parable hard to take;
they react vigorously against the injustice of the eleventh-
hour workers receiving the same pay as those who worked all
day. Their sense of justice, but also their sense of human
achievement, is offended. They do not like to see idleness
rewarded. Yet the truth enshrined in that story is the heart of
Jesus' gospel. He taught that the Father loves us and has compassion for us. This love, not anything we do, saves us. This
truth comes with age. I have noticed in discussion groups that
younger members seldom submit to the point of the vineyard
parable, but older people often do. It speaks to their growing
sense of the immeasurable mercy of God, which they now
know to be their only hope.

The last, most painful, death experience we undergo is
when our religious certainties die. This is a real knockout
blow. Those who experience it do not appear to say much
about it. Perhaps it is too bewildering for words. When they
do talk about it they say that the religious certainties upon
which they have built their lives evaporate like the morning
mist. Certainties about the church, about vocation (for
religious, but also for married people), about the Mass, and,
most terribly, about the existence and love of God, simply
disappear. They ask themselves, *Have I made a ghastly
mistake? Have I been duped?* They are tempted to throw the
whole of their faith and practice away and start again on
something new. They are, indeed, being invited to start a
new life when this happens, but it is a new life based on a
deepening of faith, not on its repudiation. Faith deepens
when it really is faith, that is, truth held without seeing it to

be true, simply on trust from God. Most of the time what we think is our faith is not faith at all but knowledge based on human reasoning. Real faith is dark. It means accepting things to be true without seeing why, only because they are given to us. Deeper than that it means accepting a person as Lord with whom we do not appear to have any relationship. This both hurts the human mind and seems a crazy foundation on which to build our life. We do feel duped at times. We do have to accept that it is all true without seeing why. If, however, we let go in utter trust that there is someone there called God whom we cannot at present feel, we are led to a more glorious resurrection than we could ever have foreseen. Because reasoning powers are the most characteristic human talents we have, their death is the most painful but also the most fruitful experience of our lives. The death of that particular grain of wheat is crucial for our spiritual fertility. It leads us surely if painfully to the glory of God.

TEN

Sharing

FEAR AND LOVE

Two instincts lie within every human being and make a person what he or she is. The first instinct is the instinct to be an individual, separate from anybody else, myself, me. This is the instinct which makes us battle for freedom all our lives. It is especially noticeable in adolescents. All those battles about what to wear, who to make friends with, and when to come in at night are really about growing to be persons in their own right. It is the growth, not without pain, of the instinct to be an individual who makes his or her own decisions. Once that state has been achieved and recognized the battles die down, as all parents thankfully know. When the instinct has not been developed, the person is a slave whose life is run by somebody else; he or she has not yet become a free person. It is an important instinct, one which modern industrial society threatens all the time with the growing impersonality of city life and the decreasing areas of choice in every field. It is half of what makes me a person.

The second fundamental human instinct is the instinct to relate to other people. This is as deep as the first instinct and equally vital for the making of the person. It is what distinguishes us from birds and animals, tables and chairs, which are individual but are not personal. They do not know and love others as we do. Imagine placing three tables in a room, locking the door and going away for a week. When you came back you would find the tables as you left them, a week's dust gathered, but nothing changed; all as you left it. Suppose, however, you locked three human beings in a room with supplies for a week, and went away. When you came back, what a lot would have happened in that room! The three persons would have interacted with one another; there would be a history of the week from Monday through Sunday; a group dynamic would have taken place. Perhaps the three would have ended up hating one another, perhaps all loving each other; perhaps it would have been two against one, with changes of allegiance halfway through the week. And so on. They would certainly end the week knowing one another better, and knowing themselves better as a result. This shows the difference between an individual human being and an individual object. Only human beings have this ability to relate to one another, to give and receive signals of communication, to know and be known, to love and be loved, to enter into the lives of others and to share their own lives. It is what deep down constitutes the essence of human living: the ability to make relationships. As Martin Büber said, "All real living is meeting." So the first basic instinct to be individual is complemented by this second basic instinct to share life with as many as come into it. The two instincts are not contradictory. They exist side by side and interact with each other. Together they make a person. The fully integrated and developed person is one who has those two instincts, both existing in a strong and vigorous state. The result may at times be tension, the day-to-day tension between the drive for solitude and the drive for company, but it is a fundamentally healthy tension. Without this tension there would be a one-sided individual, unbalanced and not fully grown, only half a person.

The way we cope with our two basic instincts determines the way we cope with life. We have to increase both drives within us, allowing them to build each other up, not break each other down. This should happen naturally. What we have to do is to facilitate the natural outcome, not prevent it. On the one hand, the more individual I become then the more sharing I become, strong and secure enough to interact in company without fears. Weak persons are too timid to share, too inhibited to allow strangers into their privacy. They think up a hundred reasons for remaining solitary, some of them conscious rebuffs, others unconscious barriers like eccentric behavior or hostile looks. Because they are insecure in their individuality they cannot afford to be open in society. Consequently they put on masks for the public and behind those masks live solitary lives. On the other hand, the more a person shares, freely mixing with people, bearing others' burdens and allowing them to bear his or her burdens, the more that person becomes a richly experienced individual in his or her own right. Sharing with others makes us more, not less, individual. Contrary to what might be expected, mixing with others does not dissolve our personalities as water dissolves sugar, but rather builds them up because our own talents grow in social mixing. We become more colorful, not less. We become more ourselves by mixing in company than if we were to stay apart. Martin Büber summed up this truth in another aphorism, "Through the Thou a man becomes I." Paradoxical as it may seem, it is through our relationships with other persons that we become our unique, individual selves. Sharing and individuality are mutually supportive qualities. They develop together, not against each other.

The greatest obstacle to human growth is fear. Fear is not a sin, but it is a diminishing factor in humanity. Fear makes us shut to others, makes us refuse to take social risks and cling to the security of solitude—meeting no one is safer than meeting people who might hurt or challenge us. Fear keeps us behind barriers, ensures that we are not exposed to other people, except at the most superficial level. *I mind my own business*, people say. They usually intend this as a cause for satisfaction; they have managed to get thorough life in their neighborhood without being hurt too much and have successfully insulated themselves against what others might do or say to them. Often behind this attitude is a hurtful experience which can be explained by another saying embedded in our culture: Once bitten, twice shy. Faced with this universality of fear in society there is no point in being greatly surprised. The fact is that it is everywhere, one of the great primary facts of life. It is, however, important to unveil it as a fact, and so learn to cope with it.

There are wrong ways of coping with fear—not morally wrong, but wrong because ineffective, as well as wasteful of energy and hurtful of others. One common way of coping with fear is to bluster. This is the way chosen by bullies who try to conquer their own timidity by making other people afraid of them. We all do it, usually without thought, by instinct. Challenged at a meeting on a point we are not sure about, we become aggressive and attempt to talk our way out of the awkward spot we have been placed in.

The opposite of the blusterer is the cringer. Some people try to cope with their fear by ingratiating themselves with everyone. They cannot stand having enemies; they have to make friends with everyone, or else they have no peace of mind. This, too, is an inadequate way of coping with fear. It is inadequate because social ingratiation only serves to cover over differences not solve them. Nor does it help the fearful person to cope with his or her problem. Fear increases under such treatment. We become increasingly afraid of people when we try to agree with them about everything and avoid differences.

A third less than adequate way of coping with fear inside ourselves is to be aloof, pretending to be indifferent to issues so that we cannot be hurt whichever way things turn out. This means running away from responsibilities by pretending to be above them, uninvolved emotionally. Behind the impassive face of the commander may be a timid rabbit, too scared to make a decision, pretending to be above the battle. If this attitude is cultivated for too long, its practitioners become incapable of love. Because they have taught themselves not to be affected by disasters around them, their emotional life atrophies. It is safer that way. This way of coping is seen sometimes in religious celibates who are afraid of the opposite sex and have schooled themselves to be coolly aloof. (Others solve the same problem by blustering or cringing.)

"Perfect love drives out fear." St. John put it in a nutshell. There is no technique for overcoming fear. We cannot solve the problem either by thinking about it or by acquiring some skill. The only way to drive out fear is by surrender to God in the moment of fear. This is a leap in the dark, a breaking out of prison, but it is not done by a tightening of the muscles. We do not have to become moral supermen. It is done, from the center of whirlwind, by simply letting go into God. It is an act of trust, sheer abandonment in love to God, a movement of the heart, not the head. This does not necessarily make us feel better or more courageous. Our knees still tremble, our stomach still turns over, but we are now aware of the companionship of God. There is a divine partner to share the experience. We are "in Christ." This enables us to live calmly through the terrors, be they social or physical, and refrain from those immature responses of blustering, or ingratiating, or pretending to be indifferent, which are false and harmful to other people. Simply love God and leave all outcomes to him. This is a movement of inner surrender, a calm letting go, touching God in our heart, allowing God to touch the depths of our soul and there create peace, even though the surface remains a place of turmoil and quaking apprehension.

The perfect love that drives out fear is not a romantic emotion. Romantic emotions have their place, an exciting but essentially transitory place, in our growth. The love we are talking about is deep and lasting. It is the mainstream of human development. It is a strong activity which calls forth the deepest and best elements in us. I suggest there are two qualities in Christian love which distinguish it from passing emotion: initiative and fidelity. Love takes the initiative. Truly loving people are the first to love. They do not wait to be loved, or even to be approached. They do the approaching and the loving first. As Christians we must not say, *When you become lovable I will love you.* We must show love straight-away, to the unattractive as well as the attractive. Genuine love toward unlovable and unattractive persons has a healing and creative power in it. I have seen unlovely people blossom into loving people under the influence of love from true Christians who have, without any pretensions, taken care of them and made them welcome. This sort of love which is divine in its creativity comes from the Holy Spirit dwelling within those who undertake to love. The important thing to realize is that we all have the Spirit dwelling within us, and are therefore capable of undertaking apparently impossible tasks of loving. It is so often our lack of faith which stops us, not our lack of talent or opportunity.

Christian love not only takes the initiative and is the first to love, it also stays in the field longer and does not cease when it is no longer felt or no longer returned. Christian love is faithful. It does not say, *Now that you are no longer as lovable as you used to be, I will stop loving you and look elsewhere.* It stays in relationship, trusting in God far beyond the evidence of termination. It is faithful. This, even more than initiative, is the distinctive mark of the love which Christ expects of his followers. He could have said, with Shakespeare, "Love is not love, which alters when it alteration finds." This is the challenge to anyone who sets out to love; his or her love will be expected to persist through all the developments which the relationship is about to undergo, developments both for good and for bad, exciting and tragic. Love does not take fright at alteration, but steadily persists through all changes, which may be for better but may also be for worse. This love is prepared to undergo many deaths as the relationship develops. It is "stronger than death." Faith in resurrection after each death is what keeps it going. In fact, only the Christian faith which believes in the paschal mystery, resurrection arising out of death, is capable of sustaining this love. The reason for this is that the ultimate foundation for such crazy fidelity is found not in human history but in God. His love for us is immeasurably faithful. In spite of our sins and rejections of him, God never stops loving us. He takes the initiative in the first place by creating us. "He first loved us" (1 Jn 4:19). He persists in loving us all through our far from faithful lives. His love will be there to greet us at the end, if we have not finally rejected him. Christians are asked to contemplate this divine love, and then in the power of the Spirit to go and do likewise.

God, as revealed to us in the Bible, is the ultimate example of how to love. His greatest revelation, his most convincing Word, was Jesus Christ. Jesus is the last Word of God, the final, completed lesson for us in how to live as human beings, and children. All that we have said about love is supremely present in the life of Jesus. He always took the initiative, was the first to love. He showed this when he broke through those constraining taboos of Jewish custom which more or less absolved his contemporaries from loving certain classes of people—the Romans, Samaritans, sinners, even the sick. Jesus also persisted in loving his contemporaries, law-abiders and sinners, good and bad, even when it became clear that this persistence would mean his arrest and death. That did not stop him. He went on to Jerusalem and taught and practiced his conditionless love there, in the center of Judaism, in the Temple. His arrest, torture and death were a true laying down of his life for his friends. The source of his love was his ability to act without fear when most people around him were filled with fears. His Abba experience of oneness with the Father in prayer enabled him to act lovingly even in the face of menacingly hostile opposition, opposition which successfully cowed all his friends.

The story of the man born blind (Jn 9) reveals this. What a lot of fear there is in that story! The man's parents were afraid of the priests ("Ask him. He is of age, he will speak for himself."), so they kept out of it, dared not be involved even in the astonishing good news that their blind-from-birth son could now see. The common people were scared, too, of the priests, and avoided involvement except as excited spectators. Despite their excitement they are very much on the sidelines and mean to stay there. As the chapter proceeds it emerges that the priests, too, are afraid. They are afraid of what has happened, the implications of the miracle, the awful possibility that Jesus may be from God and acting in his power. So they begin to bluster their way out of the situation

and even blame the blind man for being a sinner and being
cured by another sinner! "Give God the praise, we know that
this man [Jesus] is a sinner." They finally say to the man
himself: "You were born in utter sin, and would you teach
us?" But the blind man is not afraid. He keeps his head and
manages to be marvellously cheeky to the priests as they
hesitate over Jesus. His effrontery, however, does not come
from bitterness or hardheartedness. He has a tender heart
and gives it to Jesus at the end of the story. His courage has
come from Jesus' own courage. For both of them, perfect love
has driven out fear. The blind man's love for his healer makes
him speak and act regardless of all the threats of the priests.
Jesus' love for his Father and the people has once again urged
him to perform an act of compassion which arouses the
hostility of the powers that be. He healed the man born blind
fearlessly, and in doing so knowingly drove another nail into
his own coffin.

CHARITY ENDS AT HOME

Jesus' love made him share his life with all those who
came to him. He was the most richly individual person who
has lived, and his highly developed individuality caused him
to share completely with his contemporaries. Christians are
invited to do the same. Today's world, the global village, invites us to undertake the Christian task of sharing to a degree
which we have not hitherto imagined. The rich-poor imbalance in our planet has now become a gigantic scandal. We
have to do something about it. Sometimes we in the West are
told that we must embrace poverty. This is an attractively
challenging call, but not, I suggest, the Christian solution. It
is true that the gospel frequently warns against riches (the
Rich Fool, Dives and Lazarus, the Eye of the Needle, the
Widow's Mite, the Magnificat) but it does not hold up poverty as the ideal, at least not poverty in the sense of destitution.
Poverty is a human ill. Not to have enough food to eat or
clothes to wear or a place to live are evils which we must
eradicate, not permit, certainly not praise. Imagine the panic

of parents who have nothing to feed their children, no shelter to offer them, nothing to cure them when they are sick. Rich Christians must be careful not to talk of poverty as if it were a good thing. It is an evil which we should strive to remove from our planet. I learned this truth poignantly. I was preaching retreats in East Africa and gave one to the priests in a diocese. All of these priests were natives of the country, assembled to listen to this visiting European. I was insensitive enough to give a conference extolling the value of poverty. That evening at supper a young priest sat opposite me. He introduced himself as the priest in charge of development in the diocese. "I struggle every day of the week," he said, "to eradicate poverty from this poor area. It is a full-time task, at times despairing. Sometimes I do not know what to do next to help our poor people and raise up their condition. It is not helpful to come on retreat to hear a priest who has just flown out from London in a jet and will soon fly back telling us that poverty is a good thing." Father Vincent was very polite, but his message was clear. I have never extolled poverty since.

The hope for our planet, surely, is the gospel message of sharing, or love. Both on the international political and economic scale, and at the personal, neighborhood level we must practice Christian love to the extent of sharing what we have with our brothers and sisters. Even if we cannot do much at the political level, we can all begin to share at the neighborhood level. For instance, the gospel tells us that those who sleep in the streets and drink themselves to death are Jesus in disguise. We must share our bread, even our roof, with them. To do so is endlessly aggravating in the short run, but quite wonderful in the long run. If all Christians shared with Jesus, whether in his disguise as someone down and out at the bottom of the social scale, or further up the social scale as an alcoholic, a neurotic or a hurting person, Christianity would become what it is meant to be: the religion of the cross which leads to resurrection, a communal feast in which we help one another grow in the paschal mystery. The practice of sharing would come to be seen as normal, not as an eccentric optional extra for a few called to it, but a vocation for the average family. From sharing the basic goods of food and shelter Christians are led to share the intangible but more valuable goods of friendship, joys and sorrows, knowledge and experience, advice, help and counsel. We like the prospect of doing this under the influence of the Holy Spirit, but I think it is a short cut to try to engage in this spiritual sharing without also being ready to share our home physically with people in need. There is something a bit phony about a follower of Christ who is willing to share with unfortunates outside his home but keeps them from his front door. This professional division of life into work for the needy at an office or in *their* homes, and recreation in the privacy of our own homes is somehow alien to the gospel. Jesus' gospel teaches us that there is no limit to love and sharing once we have set our foot upon the way. Charity, indeed, usually begins outside our homes where we meet people with fewer privileges than ourselves and set up agencies to help them. But we are not fully Christian until we invite Christ into our homes to share with him there. Charity, it needs to be said, not only begins at home, but ends at home too.

Prayer of partnership

Jesus' life and death show us that God wants to share all with us. "He did not spare his own Son" (Rom 8:32). Sometimes the way we pray prevents us from realizing this and, to speak loosely, prevents God from sharing with us. This happens when we spend all our time in prayer doing the speaking to God, when we never pause to let God speak. We forget that in the time of prayer God is in full action, loving us with his immense love, by no means inactive or sleeping. We do not stop to let this sink in. A more appropriate way to pray is to allow plenty of time for God to do the acting. He first loved and loves us. The initiative is with him. In prayer we should recognize this. One way of doing this is to reflect that most of the statements which we make to God can be turned around so that God makes them to us, and be equally true. Thus, I can pray by saying to God, "I need you." This is completely true. I need God for everything: life, breath, food, clothing, affirmation, value, love. Without God I would be nonexistent and of no value. I need God. It is also true, however, that God needs me. Because of the way he has arranged this world and this world's salvation he needs me to be his eyes, mouth, hands, feet, to be a fruit-bearing branch of the Christ vine. God actually needs me. In the story recounted in Chapter 6 God needed me to help the girl in the train. The fact that I let him down poignantly pinpoints how much God needed me on that occasion. That being so, it is good in prayer time to allow generous space to the realization of this truth. If, then, I begin prayer by saying to God, "I need you," it should be followed by a period when I listen to God truthfully saying to me, "I need you." In this way a reciprocal relationship between God and myself is set up, and true sharing takes place. This mutual sharing of need can be allowed to take as many minutes as we like—as we become practiced we can expand the time to 10 or 15 minutes in each direction, and so fill a half hour or more. Once we have prayed this way we find that the one-sided way of praying when we only talk to God is curiously thin and unsatisfying. We develop an appetite for sharing prayer in which there is space for each partner to speak while the other remains silent. It is the prayer of Christian partnership.

The concept of need is only one of many entries into this prayer. Others are trust (I trust God; he actually trusts me), thanks (yes, God thanks me and is grateful for the work I do for him), value (I value God; he values me since I am his creature, an important realization for all of us), love (we love each other). The reader will be able to think of other basic concepts around which to pray the prayer of partnership. There are as many as we like to conceive; for instance, wait for (I wait for God; God waits for me). A suspicion concerning this prayer is that it could lead to pride and a lessening of awe for God. It seems to make God equal to us, which, of course, by nature he is not. The answer to this suspicion lies in the actual experience of praying like this. Those who do so experience not pride, but an awesome humility before God; it comes to them that it is indeed true that God needs us, waits patiently for our cooperation with his Spirit and does not force us. It *is* humbling to realize that. We may think it a mistake for God to have set up this equal partnership between totally unequal beings, himself and us, but we cannot deny that he has done so. The incarnation has taken place, however unbelievable it is. Grace raises us to a partnership beyond nature.

Once it is understood that in prayer we are partners with God, reciprocally waiting upon each other, the way is open for a limitless deepening toward complete union. After reciprocal need, trust, thanks and value have been recognized, we arrive at the stage of love, a completely mutual sharing of love, even though his love is infinite and perfect and ours is wretchedly imperfect. We love each other. We surrender to each other in love, in the depths. In fact we permeate each other, for God is Spirit and fully enters into us energizing us through our whole being. We occupy the same space. We are one. This means that we work together as well as exist together, Spirit to spirit, through our whole body and all our activities. We love each other. We share together. We are partners.

This state between God and ourselves is permanent. The time called prayer is the time for recognizing it and, as it were, basking in the fact, a time for recouping energy by travelling to the roots. But time outside prayer is as equally shared with God as time in prayer—it is the time when we work together, branch and vine, to produce fruit. Wherever we go, whatever we do, we share this ineffable but real partnership with God. We merely have to let go deep inside for it to become conscious. The fruits that follow are then completely his, but also completely ours, since our action is joint action, God and we together, not separated.

The times when I personally most realize this partnership with God are the times when I am overworked. We all

have times when so much is happening that we do not know
where to turn and are tense beyond reason. These frequently
seem to be the times when one more impossible thing happens—one more caller, one more child's mishap, one more
telephone call demanding a decision. When this happens we
are ready to snap inside, give up, because the pressure has
risen beyond the safety point. Sometimes we do crack inside
and do give up. It is understandable in the circumstances. A
person cannot be expected to go beyond certain limits.
However, in God's Spirit we can find ourselves able to go
beyond our natural capacities. Some have found these times
of ultimate pressure to be the times when by simply letting go
inside themselves they experience a free floating of the soul,
as they allow God to take over. They stay in the middle of the
pressure of business, but turn to God, let him assume responsibility. This is not a withdrawal from responsibility. They
remain in the center of things, still listening to the beyond
reason demands, but God is present and in charge. In
partnership with him they continue to act, immersed in him
but firmly in this world.

    We can experience an almost light-headed joy as we sur-
render to God and find ourselves still carrying on even
though our limit of endurance has been long passed. In God
we find ourselves, incredibly, doing "all things" with an absurdly joyful heart, free from self-pity and indignation. We
continue in ridiculous happiness and apparent effectiveness,
even through splitting headaches or supreme nervous tension.
This, I suppose, is one more instance of the grain of wheat
having to die before it becomes fertile. While we are still in
charge, we have not yet died. When we reach the limit of our
endurance and go beyond it, our own capability dies. Only
after that is it resurrected to partnership with the Spirit of
God. And so in prayer, as in other Christian activities, the
paschal mystery is found to be the ultimate fulfilment of
human living. The cross of Jesus Christ remains the central,
potent symbol of our lives. The events of Calvary so long ago
are seen to be completely relevant after all.

APPENDIX

Prayer of Partnership

I sit in your presence
Upright, with a straight back.

I let you, God as Spirit, enter into me, freely flowing through
   me, energizing my whole being.
I let go into your influence, into your being.
You take over.

I need you. You need me.
I trust you. You trust me.
I thank you. You thank me.
I value you. You value me.
I love you. You love me.
We love each other.

We surrender to each other.
We belong to each other.
We permeate each other, interpenetrate each other.
We occupy the same space.

Our work is together.
Our being is together.
We love each other.

We share.